SINCE JESUS PASSED BY

by

Charles Frances Hunter

Published by
Time-Light Books
Van Nuys, California

All Scripture quotations are
taken from The Living Bible,
Tyndale House Publishers,
except where otherwise stated.

Second Printing

©Copyright 1973 by Charles ♥ Frances Hunter
Published by Time-Light Publishers
Division of Bible Voice
P.O. Box 3521, Van Nuys, CA 91407

SINCE JESUS PASSED BY

Table of Contents

Other Hunter Books

We've probably had more excitement writing this book than any other one we've written. Why? Because of the glorious new things God has been doing in our ministry. Not only have we had the thrill of living through these "happenings" the first time, we've had a second chance to relive them as we've read the letters which have been pouring into our home, confirming what happened. We have cried tears of joy at each confirmation.

Every book should have a divine purpose, if written by a Christian author. All our other books have a specific purpose and a reason for having been written. This book is literally poured through us as we bring you our reaction to this current great move of the Holy Spirit. All the stories in here are for one purpose—to show that the miracle working power of God is still available.

The people whose lives were affected agree that there's a tremendous change SINCE JESUS PASSED BY with his miracle power! May this bless your life in a new way!

Charles ♡ Frances

Chapter 1

I WILL POUR OUT MY SPIRIT....

God said it, and we believe it!!! Never have we been so convinced that we are living in the last days as we see the power of God poured out more and more. Recently the Lord said, "I am pouring out my Spirit in the greatest manner ever, starting at the northeast and the southeast and sweeping across the entire nation!" Again . . . God spoke in a unique way to evangelist Ken Copeland and said "In 1973 the miraculous will become commonplace!" Imagine, if you can, the miraculous becoming commonplace!

Would we have believed this a few years ago? No!! Do we believe it today? We certainly do, as we have seen the power of the Holy Spirit become so strong that men, women and children have come crying out of the audience saying "I never believed before, but I do now; ask God to save me!" The above is happening in the greatest Holy Ghost Revival ever seen. What exciting times to be living in! Miracles were commonplace when Jesus walked the earth, and exactly the same things are happening today. Praise God we're right in the middle of it.

The present day revival is assuming gigantic proportions! Crowds are thronging more and more to hear the Good News. Charismatic meetings are seeking larger and larger meeting places! People are being turned away because of unanticipated crowds.

God is bringing the miraculous into focus again as all the gifts of the Spirit are being revived by His Power!

One of the most exciting things about this Holy Ghost explosion is that it could be loosely described as a masculine revival. For years, many people thought of churches as something consisting of about 28 sweet little old ladies, quilting or having tea parties. In this flaming new revival which is sweeping the country (and the world), men, real men, are being reached! Successful businessmen by the hundreds of thousands gather monthly at meetings to raise their hands and worship God! MEN are discovering Jesus to be the most powerful man in the entire world! MEN are reaching into their wallets and writing checks for unbelievable amounts to take the Word of God around the world. Executives of large corporations are taking time off from work to go and spread the Word themselves!

Some churches are complaining about young people drifting away. All churches are being faced with this great new move of God's Holy Spirit! There are only two choices to make when confronted with the move of the Holy Spirit! Accept it, or reject it ... it's that simple! Those accepting it have found the young people really get turned on by the baptism of the Holy Spirit and will flock to meetings in droves, night after night, week after week. This is not the former hay ride, bowling party, skating party, gimmick type appeal to young people. This is the Holy Spirit wooing them to a personal relationship with Jesus Christ. These include young people who have been redeemed from drugs, immorality, theft, hate, lust, homosexuality, occult, witchcraft, etc., by the moving of the Holy Spirit. It also includes, Praise God, those young people who have been morally stable, but now, given new life from heaven, they have become alive!

A letter received the very morning we are writing this states: "I was involved in drugs, alcohol, sex, crime, and anything else that looked exciting. I went to church Wednesday night just to raise hell and provoke the old fogies. I was high on grass and really loose. During the service I saw God heal my friend's leg. God convicted me of my sins and I broke down and began to cry and poured out my heart to Frances in front of about 1,000 people. After I received Christ as my personal Saviour, I was slain in the Spirit for about 30 minutes. When I got up I knew I was a new creature in Christ Jesus, delivered from drugs, alcohol, sex, crime and even witchcraft. I was baptized with the Holy Spirit, spoke in tongues and have used my prayer language every day."

We remember this young man so well! And note what it was that broke through his sin veneer! It was a miracle! It was the healing power of God in today's world that did it, as he saw his friend's leg healed. It wasn't talk about hayrides and a "sweet baby Jesus" that did it—it was the awesome power of God in the NOW! Hallelujah!

One of the most unusual situations concerns MONEY! God is doing a supernatural thing these days with dollars! Most churches complain about budgets and the lack of money. Churches where the Spirit of God is allowed to move freely never seem to have budget problems. We have seen this in churches across the nation! The charismatic churches always seem to meet their budget. The Full Gospel Business-men's Fellowship always seems to have their needs met! It seems when you're caught in the flow of the Holy Spirit's move you enjoy giving your money to God's work. In the church we attend, $50,000 was needed to build a balcony, and the pastor merely stated he didn't feel we needed a building fund program! He said he felt that God would give him 50 men in the congregation to give $1,000 each! Probably no more than 10 sentences were devoted to raising this amount, and the balcony appeared in a few month's time. And Praise God, before it was completed, the 300 additional seats were already filled!

One of the most beautiful facets of the jewel that God is putting together these days is that it encompasses every single denomination. There is not a single one which has to hang its head and cry, "We have not been touched by this move of the Holy Spirit!" God has poured out His Spirit without regard to who we are. God isn't breaking down the denominational walls either! Christians are receiving the Holy Spirit and returning to their own churches. The Baptists are still Baptists. The Methodists are still Methodists. The Lutherans are still Lutherans. The Catholics are still Catholics, and right down the line. The Holy Spirit is not trying to go through closed doors. He is going right through the denominational walls, just as Jesus went through the walls after His resurrection. "Then the same day at evening, being the first day of the week, when *the doors were shut* where the disciples were assembled for fear of the Jews, came Jesus and stood in the midst, and saith unto them, Peace be unto you." John 20:19 (KJV) "And after eight days again his disciples were within, and Thomas with them: then came Jesus, *the doors being shut*, and stood in the midst, and said, Peace be unto you." John 20:26 (KJV)

God is pouring out His Spirit in many home prayer meetings. We've just got to share with you about our "home" prayer meetings. We started off about a year and a half ago with 10 people present at our first meeting. We're not home often enough to have them with any regularity, but we try once a month to have a get-together. A few months ago we had more than 123 in our home, and decided that was too many, so by faith, we went out and rented a motel. More than 400 attended! Last month, MORE THAN 600 CAME! We're having another one next week. We have discovered a tremendous hungering among every denomination to see a LIVING JESUS! Last month a young man came who had read one of our books and had written a song about it. The Holy Spirit directed us to let him sing it, and as he sang, people began being healed all over the audience. He sang the cnorus several times, and somewhere between 15 and 20 people were healed just during the song. Hallelujah! (And he'd never been to this kind of a meeting in his life before!) Dope addicts have been freed, homosexuals have been delivered, and people saved by the scores at every prayer meeting. And praise God, at every meeting people receive the Holy Spirit and fall under the power!

This should be happening and is happening in churches all over America. This is the New Testament Church in the NOW! The Holy Spirit is moving in greater ways than ever before. Recently in the Seattle-Tacoma area, hundreds fell under the power at every service. Two of Charlie Price's daughters were at one of our services and said they hadn't seen anything like this since their Daddy died. The healings came so rapidly we couldn't even keep up with them as the Holy Spirit touched cancerous lumps in breasts and they instantly disappeared; a foot that had been crushed in the wheel of a motorcycle was miraculously put back together again and made completely whole, only by a supernatural miracle of God. Two diamond rings were returned to a jeweler after a woman heard a talk on "honesty" given by Frances. A woman walked out of a wheelchair at a retreat! A cross-eyed girl had her eyes straightened in less than 5 seconds. A pastor's wife came out of a severe nervous depression she had been suffering from. Almost hysterical, she knew she was going to "die" when I prayed for her. And die she did, but it was a beautiful death as she died to self while under the power of God, and came up a beautiful smiling woman again in love with her husband.

Phoenix, Arizona saw an ear drum restored, and much arthritis miraculously healed! Cleveland, Ohio—Dundee, Michigan—Toledo, Ohio—the power fell everywhere we went! We saw more unusual diseases healed than we even knew existed! A woman with eyelids which hadn't opened for more than a year, but fluttered 24 hours a day, went under the power and when the power went out of her body, the problem left, and her eyes were made perfectly whole. A woman with rheumatoid arthritis was healed instantly under the power!

Hundreds and hundreds are receiving the baptism with the Holy Spirit in every meeting! In Dundee, Michigan, more than 400 received the Holy Spirit in the two days we were there! But the most beautiful part of the entire move of the Holy Spirit is the way people are accepting Jesus Christ as their Saviour and Lord. There is nothing like a miracle service to bring people to an awareness of a LIVING JESUS! Many come as "scoffers" and leave with a "born again" experience. God's power is the convincing agent! We cannot help but feel the time of Jesus' return is sooner than any of us anticipate as He continues to draw His body together!

In Lubbock, Texas, where we conducted a miracle service at a charismatic conference, a newspaper reporter covered the meeting. Here are some of the quotes:

"Following a standing ovation for the speakers, a smiling woman in a white, ruffled blouse, Frances, and her dignified looking CPA husband, Charles, began their ministry.

" 'Any miracle you see tonight is because the power of God has zeroed in' she explained. 'We're two ordinary human beings . . . using the power of God . . .there's a steady stream of power through here and if you need healing, just reach up and claim it.'

". . . The people they touched usually fell backward but were caught before they reached the floor. They prayed for healing—from brain tumors to deafness. One woman who said she had been healed instantly came forward, claiming although the insides of her ear had been removed during an operation she could now hear. As they prayed for those afflicted with arthritis, a dark-haired woman

12

nearby stood up, slowly bent her knees, and with an expression of surprise, pursed her lips, closed her eyes and smiled. 'I have had pain in both knees,' she later said, 'and now it's just gone!' Another man bent over and touched his toes. 'I couldn't even do that before I had arthritis,' he told the audience, which laughed heartily.

" '. . . How many of you are still addicted to that dirty, nasty, filthy habit that ruins the Christian witness. . . .' A member of the choir testified that he had been prayed for almost a year ago and had not touched a cigarette since. Mrs. Hunter told those who wished to stop smoking to 'step out of your seats and bring your cigarettes forward—and bring your cigarette lighters too.' She prayed . . . and after the prayer she touched each person, and one by one they fell backwards, falling along the front and in the aisles.

". . . The tall woman carrying Jennifer walked forward. Again, the child's leg braces had been removed. The mother handed Jennifer to Frances who urged the audience to pray as it had never prayed before—in a concerted effort—this time with all hands pointing to the child.

"A sea of arms bathed in a soft light reached out. Each person prayed in his own way for the smiling girl. After the prayer, Mrs. Hunter handed Jennifer back to her mother and took up another child. As the mother backed towards the pews she stopped and crumpled to the floor. Someone took Jennifer. A cover was thrown over the mother's legs. Bringing attention once again to Jennifer, Mrs. Hunter asked if Jennifer would try to walk to her. She nodded and smiled, and in her halting, dancing steps, walked to the woman's arms. A surge of 'Hallelujah, praise the Lord' escaped lips all over the sanctuary. Putting the child back on her feet, Mrs. Hunter asked her to walk one more time. Taking three halting steps forward, Jennifer fell lightly against Frances. A woman in the doorway turned to the man beside her and asked,

'Could the little girl walk before tonight?' 'I don't know,' he replied, 'but praise the Lord, she's walking now.' "

How we praise God that newspaper reporters (who are supposed to be cold hearted) can see the beauty of this hour when God is pouring out His Spirit! And how we praise God that people who have been nominal church members for years are accepting Jesus as their personal Saviour and Lord! Even the unchurched are being caught up in the excitement of the moment and are crying "God, save me!" How we praise Him for this great outpouring, and how we praise Him for letting us be right in the middle of it. We don't understand it, but we don't question it. We merely accept what God is doing in these last days!

God is pouring out His Spirit in these last days in unusual ways! We've looked back at the "old time" revivals and said, "God, send us a revival—just like in the days of Finney, or Moody, or Wesley, or Luther" or some other well known Christian soul winner or evangelist. Jesus has no "rear view" mirror! Let's go forward! Look at what God is doing TODAY!

People's natures have never changed—the old sin nature is still there. Oftentimes ways of reaching them have changed. Look all the way throughout the Old Testament at the way God treated people.

He sent manna to the Israelites in the wilderness. Did He ALWAYS use this particular method to convince people of His reality and His power and presence? No, He used this only until they reached the Canaan land!

Read the story of Balaam in Numbers 22:20-35. God used a donkey to speak to Balaam. Does God always do it this way? Does He always use donkeys? Truthfully, he has never communicated to us via a donkey, but this doesn't mean it wasn't of God because it's never happened to us, does it?

God used Moses' rod to show his power in unusual ways. Do you remember how God had him throw it on the ground and it became a serpent? Do we believe

14

this is true? You can be sure we do! Has God ever given us a rod to throw on the ground and turn into a snake? No, He hasn't yet, but just because it hasn't happened in our ministry is no sign that we don't believe this story. And just because it hasn't happened to us in no way makes us assume it "couldn't happen!"

God's power turned water into blood (Exodus 7:20), covered the nation with frogs (Exodus 8:6), infested the nation with lice (Exodus 8:17), sent swarms of flies (Exodus 8:21). The Red Sea opened as an escape for the Israelites as the rod was stretched forth (Exodus 14:21).

To date He's never covered any congregation where we've spoken with frogs because they wouldn't believe. He's never infected our meetings with lice, but we believe He did it just as the Bible describes it. Do we give the devil credit for any of these actions just because it hasn't happened to us? No, we give God the glory because He chooses different means with different people. And He never runs out of unique ideas.

In Joshua the 10th chapter as God was manifesting His mighty power He destroyed the enemy with a great hailstorm. God's never done that for us yet!!!

"As the men of Israel were pursuing and harassing the foe, Joshua prayed aloud, 'Let the sun stand still over Gibeon, and let the moon stand in its place over the valley of Aijalon!' And the sun and the moon didn't move until the Israeli army had finished the destruction of its enemies! This is described in greater detail in The Book of Jashar. So the sun stopped in the heavens and stayed there for almost twenty-four hours! There had never been such a day before, and there has never been another since, when the Lord stopped the sun and the moon—all because of the prayer of one man."

Has God done that for you yet? If not, does it in any way take away from the awesomeness and variety of God's power?

15

Many other interesting manifestations of God's power are told in these stories:

... the Angel of Jehovah appeared to him (Moses) as a flame of fire in a bush (Exodus 3:2).

Sarah laughed when God said He would give Abraham and her a baby when she was 90 years old. But He did! This hasn't happened to us yet—PRAISE THE LORD!!! But then we're not 90 yet either!

Elijah and Elisha each struck the water with the cloak and it parted (2 Kings 2:8,13).

Bad water was healed as Elisha threw a bowl of salt in it (2 Kings 2:20-21).

Each of these methods was of God and used for a specific reason and at a specific time. Today God is using different methods, all unique! And all so beautifully displaying His holy power.

One supernatural phenomenon by which God is showing His power and performing miracles today has been termed "falling under the power" or sometimes "slain in the Spirit." We do not pretend to understand this supernatural manifestation of God's power, but have accepted it as a current demonstration of God's power. The first time it ever happened to us was shocking! While we were praying for a woman at the altar, there came the feeling that she "wasn't there any more." We opened our eyes, and sure enough, she "wasn't there any more." She had been touched by the power of God and was lying on the floor.

A short time later, this recurred. Again, only once during a service! Then a few months later it happened again. Each time it came as a complete surprise to both of us. Neither of us felt any special anointing, nor any "power" in our hands. NOTHING! But God didn't care whether or not we felt anything. He had a work to do, and He did it!!!! What the work was, we still don't know, but God did!

Then came February 27, 1973, El Paso, Texas. The power of God fell in a mighty way. The power could almost be heard crackling as a Southern Baptist

Church had its own day of Pentecost. Somewhere around 100 people fell under the power of God. Probably the most surprised of all the people there were the Hunters. We had never seen anything like this happen in our ministry and certainly couldn't understand it, but we discovered an interesting fact. GOD OFTEN DOES A SUPERNATURAL WORK IN HEALING, DELIVERING OR CLEANSING WHILE A PERSON IS UNDER THE POWER.

Watch what happened in the life of a married couple. God had put a call on the man's life about 21 years previously. He had turned his back on God and had literally spent 21 years in what he defined as hell because of knowing He had turned God down. He simply asked, "Could God forgive me after all those years?" We both answered, "Yes" immediately. He prayed the sinner's prayer, was gloriously saved and the power of God touched him. Immediately he fell backwards to the floor. His wife ran up and said, "It's all my fault. I was the one who kept him from answering God's call. I'm so full of hate, bitterness and resentment, I don't think God could forgive me. Do you think He would?" We assured her there was nothing that God wanted to do more than to forgive her. She asked His forgiveness, then asked Jesus to come into her life and fill her with so much love that hate and resentment could never come back into her life again. As soon as she finished praying, she too, fell "backwards to the ground" and we were amazed at what happened to her. The entire time she was "under the power" her eyes were wide open, without blinking. After about an hour and 45 minutes she got up and immediately said, "Was I under the power a long time?" Someone told her the approximate time and she said, "I thought so, because God had a tremendous amount of sin to wash out of my life." Cleansed, purified and made whole, she literally saw God washing all the sin out of her life, changing attitudes while she was under a "spiritual anesthetic." Hallelujah!

17

We ran for God's Word to find scriptural backing for this!

Look at Peter in Acts 10:9-15. "The next day, as they were nearing the city, Peter went up on the flat roof of his house to pray. It was noon and he was hungry, but while lunch was being prepared, HE FELL INTO A TRANCE. He saw the sky open, and a great canvas sheet, suspended by its four corners, settle to the ground. In the sheet were all sorts of animals, snakes and birds (forbidden to the Jews for food).

Then a voice said to him, 'Go kill and eat any of them you wish.'

'Never, Lord,' Peter declared, 'I have never in all my life eaten such creatures, for they are forbidden by our Jewish laws.'

"The voice spoke again, 'Don't contradict God! If he says something is kosher, then it is.' "

God had a special message to deliver to Peter at this time, and He did it in a special way. There was no one else on the roof with him, so there was no outside influence, and God wanted his undivided attention because He had a very special message for him. Webster's dictionary has many different definitions of the word 'trance,' such as: "1. a half-conscious state as between sleeping and waking. 2. A dazed or bewildered condition. 3. A fit of complete mental absorption or deep musing." Peter obviously was not dazed or bewildered, but he could have fit into the other two categories very well, especially "a fit of complete mental absorption or deep musing." Peter was going on a trip for the Lord and his mind was completely spiritualized, therefore capable of complete mental absorption and deep musing. God had a message for Peter and Peter alone, so he could be called "under the power" as God instructed Him that the Jews and Gentiles were to be treated alike.

Again, let's look at Acts 22:17-18. This was concerning Paul: "One day after my return to Jerusalem, while I was praying in the Temple, I FELL

INTO A TRANCE AND SAW A VISION OF GOD SAYING TO ME, 'Hurry! Leave Jerusalem, for the people here won't believe you when you give them my message.' "

Again, God had a very important message to deliver. A real warning to Paul, so He chose a unique way to deliver it. Notice that when these two great men of God went into a trance they were both concentrating on God. Peter had gone up on the roof to be alone with God, and Paul was in the Temple praying. While in this spiritual atmosphere, they were open to God's power. Their spirits were yielded to Him and they were open to whatever He had for them.

We began a search throughout the Bible looking for some additional scriptural backing for this supernatural phenomenon . . . and we didn't have to go far. By the time we got to Genesis 2:21, we saw the first example of someone who had gone under the power of God: "Then the Lord God caused the man to fall into a deep sleep, and took one of his ribs and closed up the place from which he had removed it, and made the rib into a woman, and brought her to the man." God did some real spiritual surgery the first time anyone went under the power, because as a result, woman was created!

Look at someone the next time you see them under the power! They will often look as if they are in a trance, or a deep sleep! Exactly as the Bible says! An excerpt from a recent letter to us states, "I felt a sensation through my entire body and I went backward to the floor AS WHEN A PERSON FAINTS. Just for an instant I was out and then I was aware of everything going on around me—however I was still with Jesus in spirit because I could not move a muscle in my body. It was the most wonderful feeling of relaxation I have ever known and thinking about it later the only way I could explain it to others was I felt I had experienced death to my immediate body and was raised anew. *I had com-*

pletely died to self and the body that rose from the floor was no longer mine, but Christ's."

Look at what happened to Saul on the road to Damascus! Struck by the mighty power of God. And his whole company went under the power too! (Read Acts 26:12) Read again the story of Jesus in the Garden of Gethsemane. (John 18:1-6) Again, they could not stand up against the awesome power of God!

Apparently God does not reserve this power to be used on the unsaved or just the saved, because you will notice the power was used on both. Certainly not on just those who were persecuting Jesus, because Paul and Peter were both in spiritual conditions when this supernatural phenomenon occurred! God doesn't reserve it for the "saved" because the Roman soldiers who came looking for Jesus were certainly not saved. The Bible doesn't record what happened to them, but I wonder if they were ever the same after that!

We are sharing with you some of the things that have happened in our services as we have seen the power of God touch hundreds in a single service. Some people "saved and unsaved" have apparently no physical sensation of any kind, nor any special word from God; others do! We do not pretend to know or understand what God does at a particular time. Some have stayed under the power for hours. Some have stayed for just a split second!

In Tacoma, Washington, a very unique thing happened. A young boy came forward and said, "I have no idea why I'm here!" We said, "Are you saved?" He answered "No, and you're not going to push me over either!" We asked him if he recognized that he was a sinner and that God wanted to save him! He answered, "Yes," and then prayed the sinnner's prayer. We touched him lightly and said, "Jesus, bless him." Instantly he fell under the power. We didn't talk to him again that evening because we were ministering to the needs of others. The next day, however, a telephone call brought us some interesting news. This belligerent young man who had stood there with his legs spread apart and his hands tucked in his pockets claiming, "You're not going to push me down," had cried out to God, "Save me." While he was under the power, he said a cloud floated over him. When the cloud was centered over him, it opened, and a bright light was reflected in back. Instantly he heard a voice saying, "Danny, I heard you when you called!"

Danny will never forget the night he was saved, and I do not believe he will ever forget that he was saved because of the uniqueness of his special moment of salvation. God had something special to do in his life, and He did it in a special way. Notice in Matthew 17:5 how God introduced Jesus: "But even as he said it, a bright cloud came over them, and a voice from the cloud said, "This is my beloved son, and I am wonderfully pleased with him. Obey him."

Which of us understands the mind of God? We most certainly do not. We do not understand why He chooses to move in our services in the particular way He does, but we praise His Holy Name for what He does. We praise Him for the way He changes lives. We praise Him for the way He uses this unique method of bringing grown men sobbing to the altar for salvation. When they see the awesome power of God, the Holy Spirit quickens hearts and grown men break down and cry. Hallelujah!

A very unusual thing happened in one of our services in West Texas. God is still using us in the lives of people who have felt a call to a holy life and who are still bound by cigarettes or cigars, pipes—even snuff! We had been sharing how God had caused a couple of women at a luncheon to get violently ill because they had ignored His warning in I Cor. 3:16-17: "Know ye not that your body is the holy temple of God, and him who defiles it, I will destroy!" The meeting was in a high school auditorium. A man was seated about the fifth row from the back. He let out a swear word and got up to leave. He made it as far as the aisle when the power of God hit him and he fell on the floor. He tried to get up. All of his cowboy muscles were to no avail. He tried the second time! Then the third time! Finally he lay still for a moment and God said to him, "When you promise to go to the car and get that carton of cigarettes and take them to the front, I'll let you up!" He agreed, obeyed God, and was instantly delivered from the slavery of cigarettes.

Falling under the power had a different effect on another man! The wife in this case had received the baptism, but the husband had not. He came to a miracle service and fell under the power. He said, "Nothing happened!" Then he appeared at another miracle service in another city. He wondered why he had not received the Holy Spirit. We said, "You were 'slain in the Spirit' in Pittsburgh." He said, "Not really. I just didn't resist and I just let go." God let us know immediately that He had done this for a purpose, so quickly we said, "That's all you need to do to receive the Holy Spirit. Just let go, yield everything to God and just begin praising Him, but not in English. Just "let go!" Hc did exactly that! He "let go" and was immediately baptized with the Holy Spirit. Jesus did His part as soon as our brother did his part.

Why do we want to give Satan credit for so many things? Why do some people say that praying in the Spirit is of the devil? As Charles was coming home from work one night, he was praying in the Spirit as he drove along. He just looked up and said, "Jesus, would you tell God how much I love him?" The glory of God just filled the car and he wept as he was driving along. He started praying in the Spirit again, just unreservedly worshipping God. He said the love in the car was beautiful as the Holy Spirit within him was praising God in ways he could have never done on his own. All of a sudden he stopped praying and said "Jesus, how could anyone say this is of the devil? Would Satan ever give us anything that would make it possible for us to worship God in such a beautiful way?" Then he said, "God, even if it was just gibberish, anything that lets me love you this way would have to be good." There is no doubt in our minds that it's a gift from God.

We're amazed that someone hasn't accused Jesus of witchcraft because of His ability to be "in" a place without coming through the door. God showed His mighty power through Jesus in many ways, and He's doing the same thing today in many other ways, so let's give God the glory.

In many of our services where we've seen as many as a thousand people fall under the power of God, lives have been dramatically changed, healings occurred by the scores, dope addicts have come running to God asking for deliverance, alcoholics have come to feel the warm presence of God's love, hardened sinners have been broken by the awesome display of God's power and have been saved.

". . . Don't believe me unless I do miracles of God. . . ." (John 10:37) "The proof is in the miracles I do in the name of my Father." (John 10:25) "In solemn truth I tell you, anyone believing in me shall do the same miracles I have done, and even greater ones, because I am going to be with the Father." (John 14:12-13) ". . . And the disciples went everywhere preaching, and the Lord was with them and confirmed what they said by the miracles that followed their messages." (Mark 16:20)

We have believed these Scriptures since Jesus became real in our lives, but often wondered why so few miracles happened. We had prayed for probably 10,000 people and only on rare occasions were people healed, maybe ten or twenty, and then we were honestly surprised. But obediently we kept on praying. Then a miracle happened! God got rid of our hang-ups concerning the Holy Spirit. We received Him in His fullness, and then miracles began to happen! More and more people began to be healed as we prayed for them.

Run with us, will you, through some of the exciting Holy Spirit events in our lives. Watch some of the ways God is pouring out His Spirit in these last days. Read about people from YOUR denomination who have experienced these miracles. Then let's be a part of this Holy Ghost Revival—let's not stand on the sidelines and close our eyes and say, "It isn't happening!" Let's believe that God's power has never weakened—let's believe that it's stronger than ever before! Let's believe that these things can happen to everyone! Even you!

Chapter 2

HOLY GHOST REVIVAL IS HERE

"I would love to see the whole front of my church filled with people 'slain by the power of God!' "

This was a statement from Bob Lewis, pastor of a Southern Baptist Church in El Paso, Texas, and it was from his heart. God wants to give us the desires of our heart, so be careful what you pray! See how God answered his prayer!!!

He had attended a Saturday night meeting of the Full Gospel Businessmen's Fellowship where we had spoken and ministered. He had come because we were scheduled to be in his church Sunday through Tuesday night. He witnessed a demonstration of God's power which he hadn't seen before. He didn't know it, but neither had we! Many accepted Jesus as Saviour, many were healed. Many received the baptism with the Holy Spirit. Several received deliverance from dope, alcohol, cigarettes, lust, and witchcraft, but something new was added to our ministry that night! God had anointed our hands! Probably eight or ten people fell under the power!

Sunday night in his church we shared on total commitment—giving ALL to Jesus and letting Him have freedom to do as He wished in our lives. This is one of our favorite talks, because it emphasizes the need for the Christian to stop being lukewarm, and to get rid of the little hang-ups that keep us from the abundant life. Many deep commitments were made.

25

We had completed the service and were sitting in back of the pastor as he dismissed the congregation. Suddenly God spoke to both of us and we quickly said to each other, "Did God just speak to you?"

We both said, "Yes!"

Then at the same time we both said, "What did He say to you?"

And we both answered, "He said to announce a miracle service for Tuesday night!"

Charles said to Frances, "Is that what He said to you?"

Frances said to Charles, "Is that what He said to you?"

Both of us were shocked because we had never had a miracle service in our entire ministry, and yet here was God telling us to get up and announce a miracle service for Tuesday night. Looking back now we wonder how we ever had the holy boldness to get up and announce what we did. And we still think it's a miracle that neither of us wavered as to what God wanted us to say!

Charles stepped up to the microphone and asked the pastor if he could make an announcement, and this is what he said: "God just said to both of us that we were to have a miracle service on Tuesday night." He turned to the pastor and said, "Is that all right?" He said, "Yes!" Then God put a statement into Charles' mind which was to become a very significant part of the miracles—it was just this: *"Jesus will pass by this church on Tuesday night to heal the sick. Go out and tell your friends to bring the sick, the lame and the crippled and He will heal them!"*

Now, this may seem casual, but it meant to us really trusting in having heard the silent voice of the Holy Spirit correctly. You see, we weren't in the miracle service business. God didn't speak out loud, or write a letter of instructions, or talk through a donkey or a burning bush or something else spectacular. The thought simply came into our minds simultaneously. We're both sure that at some time in the next few seconds, we must have wondered if this was our own idea, but somehow each of us KNEW that God had spoken. To make it more positive, it was confirmed with each other.

The church had announced February 25th as MIRACLE SUNDAY. Little did they (or we) realize this was to start miracles in scores of lives. The miracle they thought they were announcing was to have 500 in attendance. What a surprise was in store for all of them!

The pastor, his wife, and their nine year-old daughter took us to our motel after church Sunday night. We had shared with them some of the exciting things God had been doing in our ministry since Jesus had brought a great new dimension in our lives when He baptized us with the Holy Spirit. We felt a spiritual hunger in the family for the gift of the Holy Spirit. We said, "Would you like to receive the baptism in the car or in the motel room?" (We learned from Jesus that he didn't beat around the bush when an opportunity presented itself. We didn't either!) The pastor said, "Let's go in the motel; it will be quieter there."

We did just that and saw a three-fold miracle in a matter of a few minutes. They were thirsting for more of God and Jesus baptized them with the Holy Spirit and together they all began praising God in a new language. They just about "floated" out of the motel that night.

When they arrived home, their 20 year-old daughter said, "What's happened to you? You all look like you swallowed a light bulb!" (Luke 11:36) "If you are filled with light within, with no dark corners, then your face will be radiant too, as though a floodlight is beamed upon you." She had seen something she had never seen in her parents before, and a longing was placed in her heart for the same thing. Her longing was satisfied the next morning. She received at the breakfast table in a public restaurant!

Now there were four in the family who were really turned on. The two girls were so excited about the gift of the Holy Spirit, they wanted to share with

27

their nineteen year-old brother, Bob, Jr. They said, "Bob, wouldn't you like us to lay hands on you for you to receive the Holy Spirit?" His answer is now a standard joke in the family, as he said, "Get away from me, you holy rollers!" Bob, Jr. was a tremendous Christian, but like many of us were, for the moment he was afraid.

Tuesday morning as we walked toward the church, the pastor said, "There is a girl who has been here for the last two or three Sundays. I would like you to meet her. She seems to need love so much." As we approached her, the pastor introduced us to Mary. We extended our hands to greet her, and she stepped back as though she was frightened. She lifted her hand over her face and let out a bloodcurdling scream! Then she started to run away from us.

This really shocked us! After the initial shock, we realized that this was a demon within her and when faced with the Holy Spirit, it screamed! No demon wants to lose its abode and the demon recognized the danger it faced. What to do? We had a church full of people waiting for the service to start. God let us know quickly! The pastor, who less than thirty-six hours before had received the Holy Spirit, started to catch her. As he left, we called out to him, "We'll start the service. You bind Satan by the power of God's Holy Spirit and command the demon to come out in the name of Jesus." This sounded like we were experts at casting out demons. Do you want to know something? We had never done this before, but praise God we had read Don Basham's book "Deliver Us From Evil" the week before and remembered that Satan had to be bound before a demon could be cast out. The pastor, his wife and Mary went to the study. We started the morning service. We asked all those present to pray, and informed them of the deliverance taking place in the study.

About half way through the morning service, Bob, Jr., his sister and some other young people were called out of the service. We all prayed again, knowing the power of the enemy and how Jesus and the disciples spent so much of their time ministering to people who had demons, casting them out. Near the end of the service the young people came back into the church. We called to Bob, Jr. "Praise the Lord????" He held up a "one way finger" and victoriously said, "Praise the Lord!" We asked Bob, Jr. to come to the microphone and tell us what happened. Bob, who had stuttered all of his life said, "M-m-m-m-m-ary ju-ju-ju-just ac-ac-ac-cepted J-J-J-Je-Jesus and was de-de-de-delivered."

When Bob, Jr. completed his announcement about Mary, Charles turned to him and said, "Bob, Jesus would like to heal your stuttering. Is that OK?" Bob said, "That's OK." The prayer went something like this: "Father, in Jesus' name, we ask you to do a miracle for Bob. Satan, we bind you by the power of God's Spirit and in the name of Jesus. Father, we ask you to please go back in Bob's memories and remove everything negative. We ask you to start at the beginning of his life from the time he was conceived, and then as he was born into this world, and remove anything which may have frightened or disturbed him; as a baby up to starting school, take out any negative oppression. Father, from the first day of school or at any other time, remove anything which gave him an inferior or insecure feeling, anything which embarrassed or hurt him. Father, sweep through his entire life and erase from his memory anything negative which caused the stuttering, and in Jesus' name heal him."

Bob, Jr. said: "As Charles prayed for me, the power was so great I could hardly stand up! But I want you to know that when he finished praying for me, I was healed!" We asked Bob to step to the microphone and read something from the Bible. He read about four verses—AND DIDN'T STUTTER!!! His family came in just before we prayed and shouts and praises went up to Jesus for this beautiful miracle of healing. That night we asked Bob to share a

29

testimony. Standing before his own church, packed with many visitors, Bob said, "Most of you in this church know that I used to stutter . . ." So perfectly was this said without a stutter that a clap of joy arose from the congregation because Bob had been healed by the power of God when Jesus passed by the Southern Baptist Church, February 27, 1973!

At this point Charles explained that Jesus did mighty miracles so that people would believe he was the divine son of God, and that through him we can have eternal life. Those present were given an opportunity to make a commitment to Jesus, and many raised their hands to express that they had been born again spiritually. (See John 3:1-8)

In the meantime, Bob, Jr. was so filled with joy, and the glory of the Lord was so on him, that Frances put her arms around him as he was sobbing, crying and praising God for having delivered him of stuttering. A letter from Bob, Jr. said: "Frances wanted to talk to me and said that Jesus wanted to baptize me with the Holy Spirit. I said, 'Yes, I know!' So right there Jesus baptized me with the Holy Spirit. It was the second most important day of my life, the first being when I accepted Jesus as Saviour and Lord at the age of 9.

About 4 or 5 months before, I felt the Lord was calling me to serve him in some way. I knew that he was calling me to be a preacher and I knew I couldn't talk, so I told Jesus I would be a music director. From this Jesus taught me that when he calls a person to do something, no matter what it is, He will work it out. So now I have accepted the call of being a preacher! All I can say is, 'I thank Jesus and love Him more than I ever have before! Praise the Lord! I give Him all the glory.

(signed) Bob Lewis, Jr."

When we reread his letter, we discovered some very interesting things and we want to share them with you. His letter started off with a statement that could break your heart (if you didn't already know

30

the end of the story). "Have you ever had the problem of stuttering 17 years of your life when you are 18 years old? It is really a frustrating experience because I have experienced this. But when some people (*my parents*, of all people) come up to me on Saturday, February 24th and tell me that the next week God was going to deliver me from my stuttering after you've been stuttering this long just because they came home from hearing Charles and Frances, you just want to laugh at them. Then when they came home from the motel and told me that three of them had received the baptism of the Holy Spirit, I turned them and Charles and Frances COMPLETELY OFF!

Then Monday morning my 20 year old sister Susan and Mom, Dad and Kim went out to eat breakfast with Charles and Frances. They asked me to go, but I almost told them to drop dead. Sure enough, at breakfast my sister received the baptism with the Holy Spirit. If you don't think that this was something, it was! I didn't want any part of it! Tuesday was the last day that Charles and Frances were going to be there, so I thought that if God was going to deliver me He would really have to hurry. What I didn't know was that God had this all planned out! Isn't God good?"

When the power of God fell on Bob Lewis, Jr. and he was healed of his stuttering, it electrified the congregation! We completed the morning teaching session. Many came forward to ask for prayer for healing, and to receive the gift of the Holy Spirit. One of those receiving was the wife of the chairman of the board of deacons. And again people began falling under the power, the first one in a very unusual way!

A very attractive woman about 30-35 years of age had come to Frances and asked her to pray. She said, "I've got cancer of the bone, and my prayer group prayed for me, but I'd like for you to pray, too!" As Frances started to pray, she stopped and said, "You're healed!" The woman said, "Are you asking me or telling me?" Frances said, "I'm telling you exactly what God said to me, so let's not pray for your healing; let's praise God it's already done!" This was hard for the woman to believe, but she praised God with Frances and later told us she thought, "I'll go get Charles to pray for me since she won't pray for me!" At the end of the meeting she was the first one to go forward, but she couldn't ask for prayer for the cancer. She merely said, "Charles, Frances said God told her I was healed. Will you please pray for my unbelief?" Charles simply prayed for the spirit of unbelief to come out, and as he did, the woman went backwards under the power. It came as such a complete shock to Charles, he almost flew over her head as she grabbed for him when she fell! Soon another person went under the power—then another, then another!!!!! Many healings took place that morning, and the excitement continued to mount!

At lunch, we met another of the deacons of the church, and the following letter describes what happened to him:

"My hang-up with the baptism of the Holy Spirit was much the same as others I have talked with. I was always afraid to say much in argument against it for one main reason, I had and still have a question about blasphemy of the Holy Spirit. I was afraid that when people were praying with me that I would attempt to pray in an unknown tongue and that it would be me and of the flesh and not of the Lord. I suppose the Lord really started dealing with me when my wife received the baptism in 1972. In February of 1973, we had Charles and Frances Hunter at our church for a Sunday through Tuesday meeting. I agreed to take the Hunters to lunch on Tuesday. My wife and the other guests arrived, and I could tell by the look on their faces something marvelous had happened. They could not tell me enough . . . members slain in the Spirit, preacher's son healed of stuttering, this all happening at a morning service at our church. After I had finished lunch, Frances looked over at me and said, 'You haven't received the baptism?' After I replied no, she said she was going to pray that I receive before I left the Empire Club. Imagine that! Here we were at the Empire Club having lunch, people bustling all around us, waiters serving lunch and mixed drinks. I thought, 'Man, this is too much!' But there was no stopping Frances and Charles Hunter. For some reason (I know the reason now!) They wanted me so much to receive this gift of God. Again I was afraid to speak out for fear it would be me and not the Lord. Finally after their praying, and then praying in the Spirit, I said, 'All right, this is not for me.' I do not doubt the power of God, but for me to pray in an unknown tongue it cannot be, with six sets of eyeballs trained on me, and I was sincere. I said, 'Frances, don't you think I can receive as I walk out of this club?' I asked the question knowing that she would stop short of nothing other than me receiving. She looked over at Charles and said, 'I think he can—don't you Charles?' Charles agreed. I left, paid the check, and picked up a mint on the way out, which I always like after a meal. I unwrapped the mint on the way out the door and put it in my mouth. All of a sudden I remembered what I had said about receiving the baptism as I was leaving the club. I threw the mint down and it happened! ("Open your mouth wide, and see if I won't fill it" Psalms 81:10) What a language! This wasn't English! I was walking to my truck with this glow and heavenly language flowing, and I do mean flowing. No hesitation. I thought now I must go back in and let them know I received. I walked just inside the door and waved at the group still eating. I pointed to my mouth and gave them the O.K. sign with my thumb and middle finger. Praise the Lord! How wonderful that the Lord chose to bless me! There could be no doubt. This was from God and of God, there is no way I could do this on my own.

(signed) Dale Boren"

Isn't God good the way He treats each one of us individually? Another member of the church received at the luncheon table as the tempo of our stay there continued to increase. That night we got to the church early because we had asked the young people to meet us there so we could anoint the entire church in the name of Jesus. Excitement was really mounting, as we all converged on the parking lot. We even anointed the parking lot, asking God for a divine healing when someone stepped out of their car onto the anointed parking lot. And God did just that!!!! A 14 year old boy was healed of leg injuries when he stepped out of his car. Hallelujah!

We went into the church and probably 25 or 30 of us were laying hands on every seat in the church, every songbook, every window, every door, just simply saying, "Jesus." (Can you imagine how many times the name Jesus was said that night?) The power really began to build and all of a sudden the head deacon came rushing into the church looking for Charles. We'll let him tell his own story.

"Praise the Lord! He touched me in a wonderful way on the night of February 27, 1973, and my life shall never be the same.

I was saved at age 10 when I accepted Jesus as my Saviour and I have never questioned my salvation. Jesus said it, I believed it, and He did it. Hallelujah! For the next thirty years of my life I attended church regularly, was a Sunday School teacher, and later was ordained a deacon in our church. However, for most of the thirty years I remained a silent partner of the Lord. Sharing Jesus with others was the pastor's job because I just didn't know how and didn't have the courage to do so. Besides, not all of us are supposed to be witnesses. Did you ever think that way? Well, I did and I had myself convinced. You see, *I* was doing it.

Two years ago my wife and I attended a Lay Institute for Evangelism at the Campus Crusade for Christ Headquarters in California with our pastor and his wife. The Lord really spoke to me there and I started to be drawn much closer to Him and started

34

yielding my life more to Him. Many things have happened since then to bring me closer to Him, but there were still outside interests getting in the way of my relationship and I really didn't have a compelling desire to read His Word or to speak with Him through prayer. Something was missing and I didn't know what. I thought I had it all.

There was some talk about a baptism in the Holy Spirit and speaking in other tongues. But I knew that wasn't for me. Every time I would go to the Bible Book Store I would not go near books about that subject. When someone started talking to me about it I would become very uncomfortable and defensive. Yet, for some reason, I kept hearing more and more about it and the lives of the people I encountered that had received this baptism surely seemed different, but nice.

Well, late in 1972 we learned that Frances and Charles Hunter were going to be in our church in February, 1973. My wife had heard Frances speak once and had read all of their books written up till that time. She had shared some of the highlights with me, but I never read one book. About a week before they came to our church we received a copy of their latest book THE TWO SIDES OF A COIN. For some reason I decided to read it. I know now that it was the Lord directing me to read it. It was truly a great book and I could see myself all the way through it. I'm a slow reader, but it didn't take me long to finish it. I started to realize that what I was trying to stay so far away from was what I really needed. More of Jesus and more power in my Christian life. The idea of another prayer language sounded great. My first one didn't always seem too effective. So, I started asking God to give me this other language to speak to Him. My mouth would open, but not a sound would come out. Each time I asked, the same thing would happen. Nothing. You see I was taking a short cut. What I was bypassing was asking Jesus to baptize me in the Holy Spirit that I might have power and strength in my Christian life. That's a pretty big bypass. The book I had read clearly explained what I needed and God's word verified it, but I was trying to do it my way.

On the night of February 27 when I arrived home from work, my wife met me with a little twinkle in her eyes and I knew she had something exciting to tell me. She had been to the morning service with Frances and Charles. It had been a service where God had really shown His power to those with faith to believe. There were a number of healings that she shared with me with excitement. Then all of a sudden she said, 'and I received the baptism in the Holy Spirit.' Well, that was about all it took. I knew what I needed and wanted and was ready for everything God had for me. When I found out that the Hunters had gone to church early to pray I had a tremendous urge to get to the church. My family didn't know exactly what was happening as I rushed them to get ready so we could get to church an hour early. My fourteen year old son came running to the car as we were leaving with his shoes and shirt in hand. As I said, I was in a hurry!

When we reached church I jumped from the car and headed for the sanctuary where I knew they were. I saw Charles as I entered and headed for him. I asked him to pray with me that I might receive the baptism in the Holy Spirit. Off we went to a small classroom in the back of the sanctuary. We started to pray and as I asked Jesus to baptize me He did just that. Hallelujah! I then asked Him for my prayer language, and immediately He gave it to me. You see I had stopped trying to do things in my order and did it like Jesus wanted. What a difference that makes.

Well, as I stated at the beginning, since that night my life has changed and it will never be the same. For that matter, I never want it to be. Material possessions and sports have really taken a back seat in my life, where they used to be right up front. I used to be a casual Christian, but I no longer am. I now take Jesus with me in my daily walk and I want others to know Him. I read God's Word often now, expecting Him to talk to me through His word, and He does. Praise the Lord! I now want to pray to Him so much more than ever before, and I know He hears me. What a joy it is now looking forward to each time we can meet together to worship God rather than to feel as though it's a duty to perform. I have received faith and power to walk with God knowing that I can do everything God asks me to with the help of Christ Jesus who gives me the strength and power. (Phil. 4:13) GLORY!

(signed)L. E. (Buddy) Magers"

Things were really jumping by this time. The air of excitement was so strong it could almost be felt as a tangible thing. We knew great things were going to happen this night. And Praise God, He didn't even wait for the service to really begin! The building was jammed before starting time, and the song director started the congregation singing with the song "Jesus, Jesus, Jesus, there's just something about that name!" We were in one of the class rooms behind the pulpit with the pastor when an 11 year old girl came crying to us. We asked her why she was crying and she said she didn't know. She told us she was deaf. Then we told her it was the Holy Spirit that was making her cry, because Jesus was going to heal her that night! Little did we realize that the healing had already been done! How could she have heard us if she was deaf? We later decided her hearing must have been restored when the first note of the music started. She began to cry because she had never heard anything as loud as this. Her mother was working in the nursery, and we thought you'd enjoy her letter describing how she found out about the miracle in Carol's life.

"What do you do when you are told your daughter is totally deaf in one ear, and probably had been since birth; then nearly a year later (10 months in fact) you are told the hearing in the other ear is slowly slipping away. You pray and pray hard. God knows your needs and the right time to take care of them.

On February 27, 1973, a Tuesday evening, I was tending the nursery at the church, when a friend came in running and said, "Carol can hear, Carol can hear from both ears." I ran to the front of the church to reach her, but the church was so full no one could possibly get through. I was led to the stairs, down to the basement, up the back stairs to the altar. When I just touched Carol I knew she had been healed. She heard me call to her before Brother Bob did. She has since had an audio test and results were: Both ears are perfectly normal. Praise the Lord.

(signed) Mrs. Barbara Blair"

What a way to start your first miracle service! The singing was superb! There was such an anointing on the song director as he led the congregation; we all felt we could have been raptured right at that moment! Then he sang the Gaither song SINCE JESUS PASSED BY! The Spirit of God really flowed. He was vividly painting a picture of what happens when Jesus passes by. We were all anticipating what was going to happen. In the congregation there was such an air of expectancy we all KNEW that Jesus was going to pass by and leave results that could never be doubted.

We began speaking, and shortly after we started (and we still don't remember what we were talking about—except Jesus) a man had a "grand mal" seizure—a victim of epilepsy. We had spoken for a few minutes about God calling us to holy living and shared about the way the Lord had been using us in the deliverance of cigarettes. The epileptic came up, and almost fell at the altar. We called for a man in the congregation who had previously had experience with the spirit of epilepsy to help us, and the man was miraculously freed! He has since moved to Denver, but the pastor of the church wrote that he had just heard that this man has not had a seizure since the night of Feb. 27th when the spirit of epilepsy was cast out of him. Hallelujah! You could actually feel the Holy Spirit getting heavier and heavier, and the excitement greater and greater.

The next one who came forward was a young man who tells his own story in this letter:

"For approximately three years I debated the Christian legality concerning the subject of smoking—was it a sin, or was it just a bad habit? The answer was irrelevant, as my mind was set on continuing my habit.

I smoked for nine years prior to February 27, 1973, and believe me I was hooked in the true meaning of the word. My desire not to stop smoking coupled with the lies of Satan constantly retained my spirit and body in a prison of confusion and frustration, both spiritual and physical.

Luke 14:28, speaks of counting costs, and God was ready to collect from me. Sunday, February 25, 1973, Frances and Charles Hunter spoke at the Church of El Paso. The last thirty minutes of the message was directed at me, or I should say I felt the total burden of the convicting words that proceeded from Frances Hunter's mouth.

Through that message the Holy Spirit began to reveal to me part of the cost of being a Christian. I never heard the end of that message, because I was out of the church, in my car, and going home when she finished it. I had never felt so convicted about anything before that day, and all I could think to do was run.

For two days after that I prayed that God would give me the desire to quit smoking. It took only two days to get the answer.

I found myself at another church in El Paso on the evening of February 27, 1973. Charles and Frances had asked for those persons wishing to be prayed for deliverance to come to the front of the church for prayer. I had no idea that what was to take place in the next five minutes would revolutionize my entire Christian life.

She laid her hand on me, and cursed the habit in the name of Jesus, and before the prayer was finished, I was in a prone position, having what felt like a steam bath in my chest, warm, yet cleansing. It was as though I had a new set of lungs.

For me the miracle came that evening at home, when instead of listening to the devil tell me I wanted to smoke, I turned and pulled a chair out into the center of the room and set the devil in it. I got my Bible (the Sword) and began to cut him into small bits. I had submitted myself to God, resisted the devil, and he fled from me.

I found out that evening that God truly has given unto us power over Satan. Instead of being controlled by his lies, I was set free by God's truth."

Things began moving faster and faster! Several people came forward for healing and Jesus met them as the healer. Then Frances felt a tug at the hem of her skirt. The little girl who had been healed of deafness was sitting on the floor along with about 200 other young children. She looked at the little girl who said, "My friend's been healed, too!" Frances said, "That's nice, what did your little friend have?" Frances was thinking that kids are funny—if one gets hurt, the other one has something that hurts. So if one gets healed, the other one has to be healed, too! The girl said: "Cerebral palsy!" Our knees almost buckled underneath us. There was no doubt in our minds that God could heal cerebral palsy, but to do it in one of our services was beyond our wildest imagination. Frances cried out (silently), "God, help thou mine unbelief!" Then she looked down at the little girl and said, "Honey, how do you know you're healed?" With all the faith you could ever imagine in the eyes of a little girl, she looked up and said, "Jesus touched me . . . I felt him!"

Somehow we *knew* that God had touched her. We lifted her up to the platform and Charles said:

"Honey, if Jesus touched you, let's see you walk."
We waited ... and waited ... and waited. It seemed
the longest 60 seconds of our life was the next 60
seconds. Finally we saw one little crooked foot lift up
in the air to take a step, and then come down. And
she didn't fall over! Then Charles said, "Honey, do
you know what the man in the Bible did? He went
walking and leaping and praising God! Let's see you
walk and leap and praise God!" What a moment of
excitement and anticipation! Would she fall down?
She went walking and leaping across the rostrum! The
crowd applauded Jesus with a tremendous ovation!
When the little girl came back, we both laid hands on
her. She floated to the ground, safe in the arms of
Jesus, as she was "slain in the Spirit." While there on
the rostrum she began softly praying in another
tongue as Jesus met her as the baptizer.

We heard from the pastor two days later. Her little
feet had straightened out and she was playing as
normal as any other child in the El Paso playground.
... Now, for one of the most exciting parts of the
story, which we didn't know until after we returned
home.

This child had gone to school on Monday and
had heard some of the other kids talking about the
fact that Jesus would be passing by the Southern
Baptist Church on Tuesday night. They had been told
to bring in the sick and the maimed and the lame and
the crippled. This girl wanted to come because she
had been born with cerebral palsy. She went home
and told her mother what the kids had said. The
mother was reluctant to let her come "because Jesus
doesn't do that kind of thing any more." The little
girl was insistent, however, and the next day talked
some of her friends into bringing her to the church.
The parents were in for a tremendous shock, however, because the little girl said, "Mother, take off my
braces. I'm going to leave my crutches at home, too,
because I'll never need them again." And that's how
she came to church, minus the braces and the
crutches! Praise God for the faith of a little child!

People really surged forward for prayer about this time, as the Spirit of God moved across the entire congregation.

One of the most interesting letters we received came to us via an indirect route. This letter was sent to the mother of the girl who wrote it, and the mother was so excited she had copies of it made for distribution and one was given to us. We're quoting it in its entirety:

"Dear Folks:

Sorry I haven't written lately but so many exciting things have happened to us since last Sunday, Feb. 25, and I wanted to share all of them so I was waiting until they slowed down a little. However, this is only the beginning!!! Praise the Lord.

I don't know if I had told you but year before last I joined a little Baptist Church near where I was living then (on Finch). Well, since Christmas, in fact, just a month or so ago, David began going with me to S.S. and church there. The pastor is very much like Billy Graham—and the church has really started to grow since he came there. Anyway, the first of this year we planned a "Miracle Day" for Feb. 25th—that is we were going to work to have 500 in attendance for all the services of that day. Well, the week of Feb. 25th there were many, many people ill with this flu which I had told you Lynn and I experienced, but, in spite of everything we had 406 that morning of Feb. 25th. (I might add that our normal attendance is around 250.) In the morning service Bob Lewis, our pastor, told us we would have this couple from Houston, Texas, Charles and Frances Hunter, with us for that evening and Monday and Tuesday. Well, that Sunday night, things started to happen as they came and began to share with us their experiences the past four years and things, I MIGHT add, will never be the same for those of us who were fortunate to be there those three days they were there. They are truly two of today's disciples of God!!! Anyway, they declared

42

that Tuesday evening before they left we would all SEE some great miracles take place and they were right!

As I said earlier, their first night with us was Sunday night—the 25th—by Tuesday evening their last night with us, the church was so packed; people just kept coming long after they began to speak and were begging for *STANDING* room as the seats had long been filled. Then the miracles began to happen!

Mother, during that evening we saw (just for a *few* examples) a girl born with cerebral palsy healed—she removed her braces before she came that evening because she came *believing* she was going to be able to walk. Some very good friends of ours brought her. Anyway, she had to be led by a person on each side up to the altar and lifted upon the platform. (She is Lynn's age.) While they prayed over her, we *saw* those little legs straighten out some and later on she got up *by herself* and *walked* for the first time in her little life! A grown man with epilepsy began to come forward and he could barely make it as he shook so badly. He, too, had to be assisted and he, too, had this terrible demon cast out of him and walked away perfectly as you or I. Another woman received her hearing and sight in one eye. Bob Lewis' (our pastor) youngest daughter, who is also Lynn's age, had one arm shorter than her other, and as they touched her and began to pray *I SAW* those little fingers *grow* and become even with her good arm. His son, who is 18, was healed instantly of stuttering which he had done all of his life.

Well, this went on until about 10:15 p.m. (we started at 7 p.m.) and they dismissed everyone who wanted to leave; but very few left!

At this point I'm sure you probably think I have gone off my rocker, just as I remember about 15 years ago everyone was calling Aunt Winnie a fanatic!

You know, a person can be "real gone" on football, basketball, or any kind of sport and they are known as "fans" of whatever sport it may be, but let them become "real gone" on religion or God and all of a sudden "They're a FANatic!

Well, anyway, we stayed and as you know I have suffered with my allergy worse this year than I have since we moved here, so I decided—'I'm going to be healed of this once and for all tonight.' So, I called Brother Bob aside and I said I had been waiting because I felt the ones who they had been ministering to were in far greater need than I, but that when Charles or Frances had time I would like them to pray for me. He immediately said that my problem (I explained it fully to him) was as important to me as the other people's problems were to them and he took my hand and quickly made our way over to Charles. I called for David to come and stand by so he could see. I had *NO* doubt whatsoever that the Lord was going to cure me after what I had been witnessing all evening, however, I wasn't expecting what happened! When I stepped up to Charles Hunter he asked me (after I told him my problem) if I TRULY believed that Jesus could heal me, for you see, he and his wife claimed to heal NO ONE but that Jesus was doing it through them—My answer was of course "yes" and then he began to pray for me and as he touched my forehead I felt a sensation through my entire body and I went backward to the floor as when a person faints. Just for an instant I was out and then I was aware of everything going on around me— however I was still with Jesus in spirit because I could not *MOVE* a muscle in my body. It was the most wonderful feeling of relaxation I have ever known and thinking about it later, the only way I could explain it to others was I felt I had experienced *death* to my immediate body and was raised anew. I had completely died to self and the body that rose from the floor was no longer mine but Christ's! As I said, David was standing near and when he saw me fall backward (by the way, there were some there to catch me when I fell) he got all excited and cried out, 'that's my wife.' Charles said to him, 'Why don't you join her' and David said he started to lay down beside me, but Charles laid his hands on him and said 'Wait' and he began to pray to God that David would also receive the 'Holy Spirit' and at that moment David, too, fell backwards to the floor and they joined our hands there on the floor. When I came to, I asked David 'What are you doing here?'

If you have a Bible, read John (4th book in the New Testament) Chapter 18, verses 1 through 6. Especially pay attention to verse 6. What happened to us is what's known as 'being slain in the spirit.' Praise God for my condition for my baby will truly be a child of God.

My head opened and I breathed deeply and better than I have since November. I came home and threw away my nose drops and I will never need them again. I have been breathing fine ever since. About 75 others, after David and me, experienced the same thing we did. We finally left around midnight and since that night our feet haven't touched the ground, we have been so excited.

The Lord has already begun to reveal great and wonderful things to us, especially his word. I have spent an hour a day since Tuesday reading the Bible and His word has unfolded and become so easily understood to me as a child's 1st grade reader. I have read and studied the Bible a long time and never understood a lot or I should say, 90% of what I read. I read it because I felt it was the thing to do.

Well, the secret to all that were healed is that they all *BELIEVED*. As Jesus said, 'Whatsoever ye shall ask of me if ye ask BELIEVING, ye shall have it.' He also says that during the last days He will begin to call His people together and we shall see 'miracles' as in the days when he walked on earth.

I could go on and on but it is so hard to witness in a letter and by now there is no telling what you are thinking, but I hope you will share this letter with everyone you know because I want all of you to have the happiness I now have. I will try to explain more as I see each of you—that is if you don't run away when you see me coming.

The daughter you knew is dead, but the new one is Christ living in me.

(signed) Nancy and David"

The night was one exciting miracle after another. We asked the pastor and his wife to minister with us, because we know there is no power that we have when we lay hands on people—IT IS THE POWER OF GOD! They began to minister with us, and as they laid hands on people, they fell under the power! Before the night was over, we estimate that between 75 and 100 people had fallen under the power of God. More than we had ever seen in a service of ours! More than the pastor had ever seen in his life, and more than the people in the church had seen.

"I would love to see the whole front of my church filled with people 'slain by the power of God!.'"

"Ask, and you will be given what you ask for." (Matt. 7:7) . . . and it came to pass, *as Jesus passed by!*

Chapter 3

TOUCHED...
BY THE POWER
OF GOD

The story of how Bob Lewis reached the decision to say "Yes" to the baptism with the Holy Spirit is an exciting story in itself! We want to share with you how he told it, because his story could have the name of many people instead of his, and be a true story. Maybe it fits you, even if you're not a pastor!

"In the spring of my senior year in college, I became convicted and the Lord said, "I want you to go to a school where you can become a full time representative of me in a church related situation." Loving music as I did, I thought, "It's going to be a music director," so I went to Whelan Baptist College in Plainview, Texas, where I got a degree in music. Regularly, all through college, I would rededicate my life to Jesus. I would hit the aisle of the church and go to the altar because I was hungry for something I couldn't find. I wasn't getting all the answers I needed.

Way back there it seems God put a hunger and thirst for righteousness in my life, yet I didn't know how to get to it. I could not discipline myself enough when I was going to college to take the Bible and really study it like I needed to. I was taking Old Testament. I was taking New Testament. I'd make myself sit down and try to read the assignments; not because I loved God's Word. I was saved, and yet I was so cold because I wasn't really in love with Jesus

Christ. I got saved and got just inside the gate of salvation and then sat down. I didn't grow, but became frustrated instead.

When I got out of college, I thought 'Boy, when I go into full time church work, this is it!' So I got a church. I began to work, but I was still just as miserable as I could be. I did this for about five years. I wasn't finding the reality I wanted. I wasn't finding the joy and happiness I wanted. I still had a realization in my heart that I had been saved, but I was doubting. I said, 'Lord, if I've really been saved, how come I'm not happy? How come I'm miserable? How come I don't have real joy? How come my life and my witness isn't what it ought to be?' I wasn't leading more than five people a year to the Lord in those days, if that many. I wasn't getting through to them. I didn't even want to witness to anybody. I said, 'Oh, Lord, do I have to witness?' Once in a while I would share Jesus, but very seldom. Every once in a while someone would accept Jesus.

After five years of full time Christian work, I decided what I needed was more education. I wasn't smart enough; I had to have more college. I enrolled in Southwestern Seminary and went to school there for over three years, seeking education. I received a Master's degree. I'm not knocking education; not in the least. But this was not what I was needing. I had a wife and two children; I had a full time church and was going to school. I got to the place where I had indigestion all the time.

I finally got out of seminary and went to a church in Arlington. I was still not finding peace and happiness. Even though I was thirsting for the knowledge of the Lord, I wasn't receiving it. Then I accepted a call from the First Baptist Church in Las Cruces, New Mexico. Shortly after I moved there I went to a doctor and told him, 'I've got a swelling in my chest. You know the first thing I thought of—cancer!' He examined me and said, 'No, you don't have cancer. The only thing wrong with you is you've got a real bad ulcer that's about to penetrate your stomach lining.' I was chewing Chooz, I was eating Tums, I was taking everything I could find because I thought it was indigestion. He put me on a diet, and I got over the ulcer in a few months. Even though we had a highly successful music ministry, I still couldn't find the reality of Jesus. I still didn't have the real happiness and joy!

A few years ago a lady came to my office and said, 'Brother Bob, I want to share something with you. If you don't get too upset, I'm going to share it with the pastor. If you get upset, I'm not going to talk to him about it.' She began to tell me how she had just received what she called the "baptism with the Holy Spirit.' and she said that God had given her a language with which to praise Him in her private devotions. She said, 'What do you think?' I looked at her and said, 'To be honest and truthful with you, I don't know what I think! I don't know enough about it to give you an intelligent answer.' Traditionally I know what I had been taught. Then the next day another lady came into my office and shared a similar experience. She told what had happened to her life as a result. Then a young man in our church shared what had happened to him.

I thought, 'Lord, you know my heart. If I'm going to be able to deal intelligently with people, I need to know something about what's going on.' I began to read books. I read books that were for the baptism with the Holy Spirit. I read books that were against it. I studied the Bible. I got so confused I decided to go back to the seminary so I moved to another church close by the seminary.

One day after I had studied for about two years, I was talking to one of our young deacons while we were having coffee together. I looked at him and said, 'You know, if I have experienced EVERYTHING that I'm going to experience in the Christian life, FRANKLY, I'M DISAPPOINTED!' He looked at me like I'd hit him in the face. He said, 'What do you mean?' I said, 'As I read in the New Testament, especially in the book of Acts, what was happening in the lives of those men who traveled up and down that dusty road as they shared Jesus, I KNOW I haven't experienced anything like that. I am empty! I'm not blaming all this on God; I'm blaming it on me. It's my fault that I've been empty all those years, but somehow I don't know how to overcome it. I don't know what I can do about it! I don't know how to do it!

It was at this time the Lord showed us beyond any shadow of a doubt that I was to preach. I said, 'All right, Jesus, if you want us to preach then you provide a place for us. It wasn't too many months after that that a church in El Paso called us. Immediately I said, 'Lord, I've really got to go to work. I've got to prove to all of my friends everywhere, all my preacher friends, that I can 'cut' it in the pastorate. That I can do it.!'

Every night that I wasn't in a church meeting, I was out knocking on doors. I was visiting night and day. I was running my legs off telling people about my church. I was doing all I could. I would do this and I would do that. Everything in my power. I would say, 'Lord, we've got to have a big visitation program in this church. We've got to get all these people in.' Not because I was so concerned about the souls of the people, but because I was so concerned that I had to be successful. I had a point that I had to prove. We tried to start a visitation program that would really reach out. We put a board up in the hallway and started putting prospects on it. I began to PUSH and PUSH!!! I confess right now that my attitude was wrong, my spirit was wrong. What I was doing was in the flesh. I was laboring, I was studying. I was trying to prepare the best sermons I knew how and possibly could. Because I was so new at it, sometimes I'd spend hours and hours on just one sermon. You can only do that type of thing so long. I worried about it night and day. I worked real hard trying to get ahead, and became so concerned that I missed the objective altogether, and was on the verge of a nervous breakdown. I lost 40 pounds. I started taking pills when I got up in the morning. I took pills when I went to bed at night. I took pills before I ate lunch. I took pills after I ate lunch. I'm not bragging about it. I'm ashamed of it.

Then one day about two months ago I said, 'Lord, I've had it clear up to my neck. I'm sick and tired of being sick and tired. I don't want any more of it. I don't know what I can do. I don't have a teacher's certificate. I've never had too much experience doing anything except church work, but Lord if I have to get out and dig ditches, I'm getting out of the ministry. I don't want any more of it. If you want me to stay in the ministry, you're going to have to show me. I've got to know right now! I'm going to pick up that Bible and open it. There'd better be something in it that's going to tell me what to do. I've got to have it. I can't go on this way.'

I opened the Bible to the book of Isaiah, and the first thought I had was, 'Oh, what's in Isaiah for me?' I opened it to Chapter 61. Now listen to these three verses: 'The Spirit of the Lord God is upon me; because the Lord hath anointed me to preach good tidings unto the meek; he hath sent me to bind up the brokenhearted, to proclaim liberty to the captives, and the opening of the prison to them that are bound; to proclaim the acceptable year of the Lord, and the day of vengeance of our God; to comfort all that mourn; to appoint unto them that mourn in Zion, to give unto them beauty for ashes, the oil of joy for mourning, the garment of praise for the spirit of heaviness; that they might be called trees of righteousness, the planting of the Lord, that he might be glorified.'

When I got through with those three verses, I stopped. I began to cry and I said, 'Thank you, Lord! Thank you, Lord! Now I know that you want me to preach your gospel, because you've revealed it to me.

You've told me right there. Now if I'm going to preach it, I've got to have more than I have right now, because Lord, I'm not spiritually equipped to really preach the gospel you've given me to preach. And Father, if there is any more, I've got to have it. That is, if there is!' Because you see, traditionally I had been taught that I had received all that I was going to ever get of the Lord; that it was just a yielding in my life and in my heart. So I got to the place where I cried out, 'Lord, how can I yield any more? I keep begging you, pleading with you, crying and telling you that I just give myself to you 100%. What else can I do?

I fasted. NOTHING seemed to happen. I determined to read the Bible all I could. I didn't get any relief or any joy. Through it all I had a hunger and I had a thirst for more of Jesus. 'Oh, I've got to have more. I've got to be used more because I'm not satisfied, Lord. I can't be content, Father, going on like I've been going, because as far as I'm concerned, I'm going down a blind alley.'

The Lord began to show me some new truths in the Bible. I know that I had seen them before because after I became a pastor in El Paso, I had preached through the book of Acts. There were some things in there that I knew were there, but for my own sake and the sake of everyone else, I ignored them. I just looked over them. I didn't dig into them.

I finally came to the place in my life when I said, 'Jesus, I want you to baptize me with the Holy Spirit. Then according to Acts 1:8 I'm going to receive the power that I need to be your witness.' I did not say, 'Lord, I want a mighty experience of tongues, or speaking in tongues.' I did not. I said, 'Lord, I want POWER, because that's what's lacking in my life.' Power. Power to do what God really wanted me to do. It wasn't there. At that moment, by faith, the same faith with which I asked Jesus to come into my heart when He saved me, I accepted the fact that Jesus had baptized me with the Holy Spirit, and He gave me another beautiful language with which to praise Him!

I don't think it's psychological, because I cannot find any place in the Bible that tells me it can be psychological. I don't think it's of the devil because I don't find any place in the Bible where it says it could be of the devil. I believe this is of Jesus Christ and this is the reason I believe it: since I received the baptism I haven't taken 10 aspirin and I haven't had to take any medicine or any tranquilizers! I have more joy than I ever had before! There have been times in the last 20 years if I'd had some of the problems that have come up in the last two weeks, I'd have thrown up my hands and run. I'd have cried, 'Jesus, I can't stand it.' But I want you to know that I've got peace like I've never had before. Praise the name of Jesus. I've got joy like I've never had before. My wife and three children have all received the same thing. They've all been given a language with which to pray in their private devotional time.

Our home is not the same. We've got love in our home that we never even knew was possible before. The rapport between my three children and me is greater than it's ever been. 'My Dad is different,' they're telling people. 'He's different because Jesus has done something in his heart and in his life.'

I've got power to witness that I never had before. People are walking up to me and saying, 'I want to talk to you about Jesus.' I don't understand it because I've never had anyone approach me about Jesus when I went to a grocery store. I've had people call me over the telephone and say, 'I want to talk to you about Jesus!' I've had more opportunities to witness than I ever had before when I was going house to house, door to door, doing all I could to talk about the church. Recently, God showed me John 12:32 again, and it took on a completely new and different meaning: Jesus said, 'And I, if I be lifted up from the earth, will draw all men unto me.' Up until this time I thought I had to do the drawing. It was my responsibility as a minister of the gospel to reach out and draw all these people in, and all of a sudden Jesus said, 'Lift Me up, lift Me up from the pulpit, talk about Jesus when you go into a home to visit, talk about Jesus at the bedside in the hospital, talk about Jesus everywhere you go. You lift Me up, and I'll draw them in.' And thanks be unto God, He's drawing them in!

Not only can I see what has happened in my life, I have seen this happen in the life of my wife, my three children, and I've heard exciting testimonies from people who are members of my church telling how God has worked in their lives.

A man I know could give you a testimony of how his two daughters were on the outside even though they had grown up in a Christian home and had been made to go to church every Sunday. They were cold and indifferent. They didn't want any part of the church. Their mother and daddy began to pray and they got so concerned they said, 'Lord, please do something to our daughters; bring them back, Jesus!' And all of a sudden these two daughters came home one night and began to read the Bible. They began to go to church every Sunday. They went to prayer meetings on Monday. They went to church on Wednesday, and all they wanted to do was talk about Jesus. The mother and daddy said, 'That's great, Lord, this is what we prayed for, but what's happened?' And then one night the girls came in and said, 'Mom and Dad, we've got something we want to share with you. We had an experience with Jesus. We've received the baptism with the Holy Spirit and it has revolutionized us.' The Daddy told me, 'I didn't believe in that type thing . . . in fact I had taught against it for years and years and years. I prayed for God to touch my daughters, and then when He did, how could I close my mind and say nothing spiritual happened to them; that it couldn't be of God?' He said he began to evaluate, he began to study and he

54

began to pray, and God revealed to him the reality of the baptism with the Holy Spirit.

My children were not way out in sin, and I thank God for this, but even though they loved Jesus, their lives have been changed. They love Him more than they've ever loved Him before. God has done things in their lives that He's never done before.

'Ye shall receive power.' I believe I've found the power at last after 20 years of defeat in the ministry. I've seen things happen that I'd never seen happen before in my ministry and in my life! I believe we're living in the last days. We're going to see things that we've never dreamed of before, things that we never thought would happen. It's already happening because God is pouring out His Spirit. I'm glad I'm alive today, because I'm getting to be a part of something that's wonderful and marvelous and I'm not empty any longer!"

Chapter 4

THE POWER GOES ON AND ON AND ON....

One of the most exciting parts of our ministry is seeing it continue after we leave. Paul spent time encouraging congregations to receive his "much loved brothers" so that the Good News could be proclaimed more efficiently. He was constantly admonishing them to not only continue holding fast to the Lord, but to go out and teach others. "Oh, Timothy, my son, be strong with the strength Christ gives you. For you must teach others those things you and many others have heard me speak about. Teach these great truths to trustworthy men who will, in turn pass them on to others." 2 Timothy 2:1-2.

The desire of our hearts has always been to breathe a real discipleship into the lives of others. It's fun to see congregations get all excited, but before we received the baptism with the Holy Spirit, we sometimes wondered what happened after we left. Did they continue on, or did they drop back into lukewarmness in just a little while? The enduement of power from on high which comes with the baptism of the Holy Spirit calls people out of the ranks to serve God as one of those Paul spoke about "who will, in turn, pass them (great truths) on to others."

In the revivals of the past, people have often worshipped an "idol," and felt God could move only through an "idol," but certainly not through an ordinary individual. We probably thought the same thing ourselves years ago, but through the power of the Holy Spirit wherein we KNOW we have the very power of God in our lives, the ordinary layman is reaching out to touch others, and Spirit-filled pastors are discovering the Holy Spirit is bestowing the gifts of the Spirit in generous quantities to those who will ask. An "idol" is not necessary—only the moving of God's Holy Spirit.

At a meeting in the Seattle-Tacoma area, the wife of the pastor of the Abbott Loop Community Chapel, in Anchorage, Alaska came and attended almost every meeting we had in the area. She saw tremendous numbers of people accept Jesus as their Saviour, go on to accept Him as the baptizer, go on to accept Him as healer, and really get turned on to Jesus. The last night we were in the area she and another friend from the congregation were with us and God spoke to us and said, "Lay hands on her and let her take this back to Alaska." We laid hands on both of them, they both went under the power, and when they came out we asked God to anoint their hands for a healing ministry in the Alaska area. Carol (the pastor's wife) went home, laid hands on her husband who fell under God's power. Then they in turn laid hands on the elders and their wives who all went under the power. That night when the evening service was over, all of the elders, their wives, and the pastor and his wife, ministered to the entire congregation and more than 300 people fell with a special touch of God upon their lives The following letter tells some of their story.

"Dear Frances and Charles:

From the time you laid hands on me that Friday evening in Tacoma, my life, which had been busy and blessed before, just hasn't been the same. Everyone says there has been a tremendous change (Dick says he had a great wife before but she's better than ever, now). More love, more compassion, and more of an awareness of the immediacy of the presence of the Holy Spirit—in *power!* Hallelujah!

There have been many wonderful things happen in our congregation and Nita [the friend who accompanied her] and I have gone to several other churches (our branch churches and one other small community about 125 miles north of here) to spread the good news and the Lord has confirmed what we said with miracles—healings, baptisms in the Holy Spirit, deliverances from satanic oppression and possession, etc. And, best of all, we have had reports from the one branch church 180 miles south of Anchorage that the pastor and his wife are continuing the ministry and God is pouring out the blessings—this makes us very happy.

Some of the healings we have had in the congregation: a hernia went in immediately as the man was slain in the Spirit and he has not had any trouble with it since; this man was also delivered from smoking; prayed for a woman with lumps on her breast, the lumps were completely gone within a week's period— Praise God! A growth disappeared from the back of a man's hand (one of our elders); also one of our elders was healed of arthritis, *immediately;* several people have had their eyes healed and have had no further need for their glasses—one of the young men even had to renew his driver's license and now it bears the remark "no glasses needed" (State-proven testimony!); legs lengthened; *many* have been delivered from smoking; a baby's crooked feet were straightened right in Nita's hands as she prayed for them; many emotional healings (God is doing a fantastic thing as far as taking out scars on the inside of people, many times situations from deep in their past, even childhood, which in some instances, they weren't even able to verbalize or fully describe; God is taking these things out completely, and filling the person with love, joy and power—Glory. Deafness has been healed (even my own precious mother had her ears healed and can hear her watch tick, which she hasn't been able to do for at least 5 years)! Several have had beautiful, spiritual visions while slain in the Spirit—one a boy 10 years of age, which brought tears to the eyes of the whole congregation when he shared it, it was so beautifully moving and scriptural! I prayed for a boy 4 years of age with only 50% hearing in both ears—his eyes never closed but he laid back after I prayed for him. His daddy laid him on the floor (eyes still wide open and brimming with tears)—his ears were completely healed and he told his daddy 'the reason I fell back was that an angel was there and pushed me back to the floor.' Praise God. This boy's parents are from a large Southern Baptist Church here and have been marvelously touched of the Lord, too, through all of this. (Daddy's ears were healed, too.)

Dick and I and Nita and her husband will be ministering to the pastor of a large church, and his wife. They have heard about what is happening out here and expressed to some of their Spirit-filled members that 'they wanted it' and a private meeting is set for tonight—we are excited, to say the least, and anticipating what God is going to do. This church has about 40 Spirit-filled members (who have been praying like mad for their pastor)! Glory!

All I can say is PRAISE GOD—it is getting better and better! The Lord is so faithful—He has been giving me insight into the hearts of the people for whom I am praying and it has been ending up that we minister for at least an hour and a half following every evening service. BLESSINGS! BLESSINGS! BLESSINGS!

Abbott Loop was terrific before but it is super-charged now—Praise God—and I know it is only the beginning—Jesus is coming soon and He is getting His people ready for that great day . . . it is so exciting to be a small part of what he is doing.

In the Love of Jesus,
(signed) Carol and Dick

P.S. I want to share this one testimony in detail: It is

a woman who goes to a Wesleyan Methodist Church and visits our Tuesday morning Bible Class and Thursday evening service . . . She is Spirit-filled. For years she has been terribly bound by smoking.

About a month ago she was reading THE TWO SIDES OF A COIN and after finishing the chapter on smoking, she slumped back on her couch and was actually pinned to the couch. She had no idea what was happening and in her heart asked God, "What is this . . . conviction, Lord, or what?" She had no answer and dismissed the experience.

When she heard about the Sunday night service and heard that Nita and I had been in your meetings the Holy Spirit spoke to her heart and told her that the deliverance from smoking was at hand and she couldn't wait for our Tuesday a.m. meeting.

She was one of the first ladies I prayed for and was immediately slain in the Spirit, and has had no desire for cigarettes since . . . Praise God. She said it is truly a miracle as she has been tormented by the smoking habit for years and wanted to give it up but in her own strength had no success. Praise God.

Many broken home relationships have been mended, between husband and wife, parents and teenagers, etc. It has been fantastic. As Dick says, God put Adam into a deep sleep to prepare his bride, and God is preparing a Bride for the Lord Jesus and sometimes this 'deep sleep' experience is vital!

I could go on and on. . . ." [End of letter.]

Looking over some of our recent meetings we've wondered if they might not have been like some of the meetings of the New Testament Churches. They certainly don't follow a set pattern as some churches approve of (it might even appear disorderly), and to someone who doesn't understand, it might look like a lot of people are slightly tipsy. They're not—they're just plain drunk. Drunk on the power of God's Holy Spirit. Drunk on the New Wine we all need to drink!

"They stood there amazed and perplexed. 'What can this mean?' they asked each other.

"But others in the crowd were mocking. 'They're drunk, that's all!' they said." (Acts 2:12,13)

Wouldn't it have been fun to have been in the Upper Room on the Day of Pentecost? I imagine it was a little disorderly, I imagine it would have been a little noisy, and I don't imagine it followed any set pattern. I have a feeling the offering wasn't taken at exactly 11:22 a.m. Some of today's services where the Spirit is allowed to move probably look a little disorderly to a lot of people. PRAISE GOD! His Spirit is being allowed to move, and people are drinking the new wine! The power didn't stop after the Day of Pentecost. It didn't even stop when the disciples died! The power has always been here! Hallelujah!

One of the most unique examples of this occurred in the city of Des Moines, Iowa, during the Iowa Yearly Meeting of Friends. We were scheduled to be the speakers at this meeting whose subject was THE POWER OF THE HOLY SPIRIT, and the initial correspondence had some discussion about whether or not to discuss the supernatural phenomenon of speaking in tongues. Being very new in the Spirit at the time of the original booking, we just waited on the Lord to see what He would have us do, and time went on. One day we got a wild exciting letter from the program chairman who told us she had received the baptism with the Holy Spirit and her entire life had been changed, and the difference in her letters before and after was thrilling! Power was there! Joy was there! Love was there! And assurance was there! When we arrived in Des Moines, we discovered her husband had also received the baptism and his life had really changed as a result. The same things had happened to him.

> Power was there!
>
> Joy was there!
>
> Love was there!
>
> Assurance was there!

The meeting started on Friday night, well attended and the response was beautiful! Nothing unusual happened until a meeting at the pastor's house, after the service, where we were asked to share the baptism with the Holy Spirit. We spoke and shared the Scriptures which had meant so much to us in changing our minds about this subject, and that the real power from on high would never be available until we were willing to yield all, including our tongues! Neither of us remember anything particular happening as a result of this meeting. We remember one or two receiving, but for the most part, there wasn't much comment either way.

The next day they passed out questionnaires prior to the first teaching session asking the following questions:

1. What do you want the Holy Spirit to accomplish in your life this weekend?
2. What would you like the Holy Spirit to do in your church?
3. What is the most specific point of resistance to letting the Holy Spirit totally control your life?
4. What time in your life was God the most real to you?
5. What is the most valid experience of prayer you've ever had?
6. Write what is your understanding of the Holy Spirit in relation to you in 1973.
7. To the best of your knowledge and understanding, who is the Holy Spirit?
8. What is the prime purpose of the Holy Spirit in your life?

The answers to these questions can tell you a tremendous amount about a church and its people. (You might try it in your own church some time.) The Friends (Quakers) are a very committed denomination, although rather staid. The answer to the second question brought tears to the eyes of many of the people as we asked several of them to stand and tell what they wanted the Holy Spirit to do in their church. Most said the same thing: 'Set it on fire." "Get it excited." "Bring unity and love." We especially remember one older man standing up and saying the only thing he wanted the Holy Spirit to do in his church was to bring love into it. He cried and so did we. Only the Holy Spirit can bring genuine, true, agape love into a church and smooth out all the wrinkles. There was such a genuineness and concern on the part of almost everyone there about the future of their own church. They all wanted their churches to know the very fire from heaven, and they were honest in their statements. The hungering in their hearts for real revival was just beautiful! When our plane had landed in Des Moines the night before, we had asked God to pour out His Spirit in greater ways than we'd ever seen before and we heard that small still voice saying, "I will do just that!" Little did we realize what this really meant.

During our first session on Saturday morning, God spoke to Frances in such a strong way there was no doubt He meant it, so she got up and said, "God just told me to announce a miracle service for tonight! Call any of your friends who will have time to drive here before tonight and urge them to come." No sooner had she said that when God put another thought into her mind: "Tell them they'll see things they've never seen before." Frances told them just that, then she was as shocked as the congregation because God spoke to her and said, "And you and Charles will see things you've never seen before!" She repeated this to the congregation and things began to happen! An unusually heavy anointing fell on Charles and he stood up and spoke for a few minutes:

He expressed firmly and with a deep sense of urgency that the signs and wonders which would follow those who believed would be seen as Jesus did miracles that night in the miracle service. He proclaimed that these signs and wonders were happening across the nation in many ministries and groups, but only, except in remote instances, in the ministries of those who had accepted the baptism of the Holy Spirit. He urged each person there, whether or not they believed in the baptism with the Holy Spirit manifested by speaking in tongues, to observe what God would be doing that night in their church, then to re-examine the Scriptures relating to the gift of the Holy Spirit, and prepare to accept all of the power of God in their own lives. He assured them this modern "Acts" would not occur except through the power of the Holy Spirit which came into our lives after we accepted the baptism with fire and spoke in tongues.

The excitement began to build up and by the beginning of the evening service there was a great feeling of anticipation. Some had called people who came from a great distance to attend the miracle service. We were as excited as anyone because of the fact that God had told us we would see things we had never seen before. We had no idea what God had in store for us!

Word had gotten around Des Moines and the church was jammed with people from other denominations as well. We simply shared some of the things God has been doing as He pours out His Spirit, and then asked those who had come for healing to come forward and form a line on the right. NO ONE CAME! We thought maybe we hadn't worded it plainly, so we repeated the invitation. AGAIN NO ONE CAME! Finally one woman came, accompanied by two friends. This was an unusual moment! We both wondered why no one came up to be prayed for! Frances silently screamed: "God, was I in the flesh when I announced a miracle service, or did you tell me to announce a miracle service?" She was really beginning to wonder. Then God whispered, "Lay hands on the pastor!" We both turned around and motioned to the pastor to come forward. Truthfully, neither of us remember what we prayed. The next thing we knew we heard a THUD! There was Pastor Wolfley lying under the power! His wife screamed because she had never seen anything like this, and I'm sure there was some concern among the people there, but her scream was part of God's plan to remind us to let them both have the same experience. We asked her to come forward, and as we laid hands on her, she too fell under the power! We joined their hands and separated them for special service unto the Lord!

She came out from under the power first, and after approximately 30 minutes (who was keeping track of the time?) he sat up and crawled over to the deacon's chairs and managed to pull himself up onto the chair. We looked at him and honestly, all of us had to laugh. Never have we seen anyone so completely drunk on the New Wine as he was! It was the start of a real night of Pentecost, and as he sat on the deacon's chair hanging on for dear life, completely saturated in the New Wine, we began praying for others. After we laid hands on the pastor and his wife, and they went under the power, the line grew to about 20, then 50, and as we began ministering to their needs, we discovered something very unusual! Almost everyone we prayed for FELL UNDER THE POWER! And many of those who fell began to speak in unknown tongues as the Holy Spirit gave them utterance. The faith of the congregation ignited when the pastor fell under the power and then miracles began to happen.

When the pastor finally "sobered" up from the powerful touch of God, we told the congregation we wanted to show them that there was no power in us but that everything they saw happening was the power of God. We asked the pastor and his wife to lay hands on the next two people in line. (The pastor later said he'd been wondering how "we" did it.) The power became so strong that neither he nor his wife laid hands on anyone because as they raised their hands, the individual they were praying for fell under the power of God! They began to minister along with us and had the thrill of seeing a young man with back problems healed as God touched his spine, and manifested the healing with a short leg growing out to equal the other one.

We've often wondered what four could do, since one could put 1,000 to flight, and two could put 10,000 to flight, and we began to find out. God had promised we'd see things we had never seen before and He held true to His word. The power and presence of God became stronger and stronger and the love of God was so real and personal that night that no one could have walked away untouched! More and more people began falling under the power as God really began touching lives, and just as on the Day of Pentecost, they began speaking in tongues! The power kept building up and it began to look like a hurricane had hit the building because there were so many people slain in the power. We had never seen anything like it, and all of a sudden we looked up and said, "JESUS, what's going on here?" . . . . and at the name of JESUS, many of those standing fell backwards to the floor, and many sitting in their seats were jolted right onto the floor by the power of God. Many were so drunk, even at midnight, they had to be helped out of the building.

We had heard of the old time revivals of Moody, Finney and many others where this occurred, but this was the first time we had seen people just fall over all by themselves. The only way we could tell who was falling was by the "THUD" we heard as they went down.

Probably the most beautiful part of all this was the hundreds who made a deep recommitment of their lives. There is nothing like a miracle service to bring people to Jesus, and to bring those who have been lukewarm to a total commitment!

One deaf and blind old man came forward for prayer. As we prayed and commanded the spirit of deafness to come out, his hearing was restored, but there was apparently no miracle in his eyes. Two nights later we got a telephone call which thrilled our hearts. He was sitting in his living room and suddenly said to his wife, "Honey, that's a beautiful smile you've got!" She replied, "How do you know I'm smiling? You can't see me." He replied, "Yes I can!" That night he got to see his grandchildren for the first time! Hallelujah!!!

This part of the story could end right now and still be an exciting story, but even more thrilling was the afterglow. Nothing that happened had anything to do with us, it was all the supernatural power of God as He is pouring out His Spirit in these last days! We have absolutely no power of our own—the glory all goes to God! How we praise Him for letting us be a part of this great revival.

Shortly after we returned to Houston the mail brought us two exciting letters. We quote them in part:

"The most beautiful thing about the miracle service on Saturday night (17th) is that the power didn't stop flowing when that service was over. Oh, the days change and time passes, but the work of the Holy Spirit just goes on and on here. PRAISE GOD!

I'm so excited about taking our daughter to the doctor so that he can tell me that there is no longer anything wrong with her heart! But, even more than that—I thank God that my walk with Him is closer than ever before. I just think "Jesus, Jesus, Jesus!" All the time.

You know, when you had the congregation hold out their hands as though the souls of their unsaved children were being held there, I held out my hands too—but instead of my children, for whom I pray unceasingly, my hand held my father's soul up to God. This is the first time since being married that I have carried a burden for my daddy. Thank God he spoke to me about the responsibility children have toward their parents as well as that which they have toward their own children.

Tim spent the entire day at the Yearly Meeting headquarters with Marvin Hoeksema (General Superintendent) and Eugene Wolfley (Pastor, Des Moines

Friends Church), and guess what—although Marvin had to miss Saturday night's miracle service in Des Moines, he didn't miss the full blessing of it for he was slain by the power of the Holy Spirit in his office on Tuesday as Tim and Eugene and William Griggs (William Penn College chaplain) ministered in the Holy Spirit to him! What a day of rejoicing it was! That same day Marvin ministered in the power of the Holy Spirit to his wife, and she too was slain by the power of the Holy Spirit! Praise God! The general superintendent, state-wide youth director, college chaplain—the leaders of Iowa Yearly Meeting of Friends have *all* been baptized in the Holy Spirit. It pays to walk with Jesus. To God be the glory!

If you were to ask me now if I had read any of your books, I could answer, "Yes!" I have just finished *How to Make Your Marriage Exciting,"* and I enjoyed it so much! I must admit that I was convicted as I read it, because the beds weren't made, dishes weren't done, etc. And Tim likes the house neat at all times. So, I stopped reading and went to work.

God bless Tim. I need him so much, because on my own I'd be very sloppy—and that just doesn't please God." . . .'Let all things be done decently and in order.' (God, does that mean housework too?)

Thanks for adding to our ministry with the young people of the Friends churches in Iowa. God bless and reward you richly.

In the service of the KING

(signed)Frieda Henley, 'B.A.' (Born Again)"

"P.S. Thank God that He shows me *elegant* Christians—common but still elegant. I claim that for myself, because it glorifies God."

"P.P.S. FROM TIM— I'll just add to Frieda's letter. How the POWER goes on and on and on!!!! It didn't dry up! The phone hasn't stopped ringing—people from all over the state are calling to share the on-going blessings. All week more and more people have been baptized in the Holy Spirit as those who were present at the miracle service in Des Moines have gone home and have been faithful to lay hands on others who weren't there and pray for them. We just got a phone call from a couple of pastors who were baptized with the Holy Spirit last night! Hallelujah!!!

I've been baptized in the Holy Spirit for nine years—and never dreamed, never even hoped that it could happen in a large-scale way to the Friends churches. But, how faithful God is to pour out His Spirit upon ALL people!

Pray for all of us. There is that small sprinkling of doubters who would like to "have our hide" because of the new dimensions in our ministry—and we must LOVE them with superhuman God-love.

I laid hands on a young high school girl last night who wanted the baptism of the Holy Spirit, and what a joy to sense God setting her apart for His service as she revelled in His presence!

We had an anointing service right here in my office earlier this week. In Jesus' name we anointed *everything;* the chairs, the desk, the doorways—and people just get "drunk" when they come in now. WOW! WHAT'S HAPPENING TO US?

Love, in Jesus

(signed) Timothy E. Henley, "B.A." and "Ph.D."

(*Ph*illed with *D*ivine Joy)

State Youth Director"

. . . and here's the letter from the General Superintendent, Iowa Yearly Meeting of Friends:

"Iowa Quakers will never be the same after the bountiful blessings poured out during the Conference on the Holy Spirit in mid-March. God bless you!!

The baptism goes on an on and on! P.T.L.!! We have been liberated in a new found power of reliance upon the Holy Spirit. How we praise Him for sending you to be His instruments of release. Thank you for your living demonstration of the power at work in your lives.

I was unable to be present for the closing meeting on Saturday evening when the tremendous baptism took place. However, on the following Tuesday, in my office, Bill Griggs, my secretary, our youth director and Pastor Wolfley prayed with me for a slaying of the Holy Spirit. I will never (Praise God!) be the same. The power fell upon me. What a joy! What a joy I have in my soul!!"

Yours in the power of the Spirit,
(signed) Marvin Hoeksema, General Superintendent
Iowa Yearly Meeting of Friends"

Praise God, he doesn't cut off the power when the evangelists leave. We have thrilled over the numerous telephone calls we have received from the state of Iowa, sharing the on-going blessings and the great moving of His Spirit. There will always be those who will hang back and who will not believe great movings of God, but then they didn't all believe Jesus, either, did they? But how beautiful to see so many flowing with the rivers of living water gushing around all over the place in every denomination and in every state,

The power goes on and on and on . . . .

Chapter 5

JESUS,
TURN ME ON....

"Jesus, turn me on, *please* turn me on while we're out here." That was the simple prayer that Tom prayed the first morning he and his family were with us for a real "Jesus" week. In those few words, however, I heard his very heart and soul cry out for something to take him out of a defeated Christian life. He and his wife had accepted Christ in June, but their walk was very erratic. Occasionally up, but mostly down, down, DOWN at the very bottom. At times I even wondered if their lives and marriage were much better than before they accepted Jesus.

I looked back and found a letter I had written to Tom on March 10, 1971, the day our grandson David Edward was born. My heart had rejoiced as I thought about our new grandson, and yet I was heartbroken when I thought of what the little one was going to face if his parents didn't find Jesus! This is what I wrote:

"Dear Tom:

I'm so glad that you're all happy about our little boy. We're really thrilled down here. Charles is so tickled he's behaving like a real grandfather, and if he smoked, I know he'd give out cigars.

I couldn't help but pray as soon as we hung up the telephone, claiming the little one for Christ. As I think of your family now, and I do hope some day all of the kids will have the same last name, I wonder if you realize the tremendous responsibility you have. These three children (and another little girl to follow) will look to you for the answers to life until they either get turned off or something else happens. I really pray that you will want to raise them in a Christian home.

When you asked me the other morning if I ever wondered what it was all about and if it was all worth while, let me say I wondered that many times until I remembered what Jesus said, 'Come unto me all ye that labour and are heavy laden, and I will give you rest.' And this is true, because never have I felt that way since I really gave all of my life to Christ. And you made another statement which has stuck in my mind when you said as you looked back over your life some of the things you did make you sick.

You can go on, Tom, the rest of your life, letting these things 'make you sick,' or you can believe what God says when He says He'll forgive everything you have ever done, and wash the slate as white as snow, if you'll just ask Him, and then let him direct the rest of your life. With you it isn't a question of praying that little prayer in the Four Spiritual Laws, it's just a question of intellectually deciding who's the smartest—you or God! And then simply telling Him that you want Him to run your life.

If you'll look in the REACH OUT New Testament we sent you you'll discover on one of those pages I have underlined about the forgiveness of God. I honestly didn't believe I had ever been a sinner until after I accepted Christ, and then and only then did I realize how much God had forgiven me for and to this day whenever I am reminded of something, I just say, 'Thank you, Lord, for forgiving that, too,' but once God wipes it out, there's never guilt anymore, just rejoicing.

Somehow or other, I didn't mean for this to be a lecture, but when a new little life is born, we are all reminded of the fact that God created all of us in His image. Some of us have gone a long way from the original image in which we were created, but God loves us enough to bring us back. How He can ever love us so much I'll never know.

Well, please know we're continuing to pray for you, Patty, the kids and the business. We ask God to let you know how much more capable He is than you are, and we pray for a Christian home for all of you, because I wouldn't want to raise three children today without Christ being the center of the home. I just got back from a youth convention in Wisconsin and it makes me really sick to see what is happening to many of the young people today.

We love you and can't wait to see that little guy. There's a possibility that we may let Joanie come down for Easter, because I don't think she can stand it beyond that, but we'll let you know definitely.

Give our love to Wayne and Kimberly and whatever his name is, and for you and Patty a very special kind of love.

Because God loves, we love,
(signed) Charles, Frances and Joan"
(Dad, Mom and Sister)

The marriage continued rocky and the end of April, 1971, we wrote the following letter:
"Dearest Tom and Patty:

After talking to Joan last night, I felt an urge to drop you a little note about something we've discovered and I hope you will listen, and this is with no idea in mind of running your life.

Charles and I are always ecstatically happy because we've found the secret to life. THE SECRET OF LIVING IS *GIVING*. We've given our entire lives to God, we GIVE to each other, we GIVE to the people we share our faith with, it's a constant time of giving, and because of this, we are ALWAYS happy. If the two of you would just realize it is far more blessed to give than to receive, it would do something for your marriage.

Ask yourselves honestly. Do you want to make

your marriage a success, or do you want to go through the rest of your life floundering around being miserable and never finding the answer to life? Will you read to each other the 13th chapter of I Corinthians every day for the next month? This tells you what love really is, and I believe if you want to make your marriage work, this will do it for you.

Tom, you have so much love, and so does Patty, and you let the devil (and that's exactly what it is) keep you from enjoying each other and your children to the fullest. Both of you have an inborn desire to give, because both of you have shown evidences of this, but somehow or other, you let your EGO get in the way and before long, it's more important what 'I' do than what makes someone else happy.

Marriage was created by God himself to make two people into one, and when you fail to realize this and each of you feel you want to be a separate individual, the devil just brings you misery. I didn't believe in the devil until I became a Christian, but now I know how real he is.

Try it, just for a month, and as you read it, look at that baby of yours and say, "David, we're reading this for you." You might also look at two other children, too, whose lives are going to be ruined if they don't have a home where love reigns supreme all the time.

This is written only because we love you.

Mother and Dad"

Had we promised them too much? Had we promised them more than Jesus could live up to? We knew we hadn't. Then what was wrong!!! It dawned on us! The devil knew he was losing a good disciple, and he was putting up a tremendous fight for Tom and his wife. He started on them immediately! He didn't even wait until they returned to Miami after coming to Texas to share their testimony of being saved (See THE TWO SIDES OF A COIN). They took a night flight from Houston and arrived in Miami at 11 P.M.

Neither of them was in the best humor, because they had run out of Pampers for the baby. They dashed off the airplane at New Orleans to get some. They were out! They couldn't find any, so they had a "super soggy" baby when they arrived. Halfway between the airport and home, their car threw a rod, and that was the end of the car. We had put a $5 bill in their hands before they left Houston and didn't realize this was all they had. They called a cab, and it took all we had given them to pay the bill.

The devil really went to work on them! They arrived home to discover something had gone wrong with the refrigerator. Everything in it had spoiled, including the milk and all the food. The children had no milk to drink. They managed to praise the Lord (weakly I'm sure) and then they saw the mail which had come in their absence. There was a letter with the interesting information that their electricity and telephone were being cut off if the bills were not paid. Hallelujah, how many more good things could happen to them? Another letter brought the news that an account of $700 which was due them was turned down by the court, and the money they had planned to use to buy food was now gone down the drain.

Our natural desires were to send them some money immediately, but God wouldn't let us! Every time we sat down to a delicious meal, we'd praise God and thank Him for supplying their needs somehow. And that's exactly what He did. Each time they got desperate, money turned up from somewhere to fill their stomachs. Occasionally we would put a little something in a letter to make life a little easier for them. We talked to them often, to get the pulse of the situation, and tried to encourage them to keep praising the Lord anyway, regardless of what happened. We also told them to rebuke the devil and send him fleeing from their lives. Looking back now I wonder sometimes how they kept hanging on.

But God was working throughout all of this, teaching them to give thanks for ALL things, and teaching them to trust Him (and not their parents) through all situations. Sometimes the lessons we have to learn are hard!

Little changes were being made in their lives, changes so gradual at times it was hard to see they were there. One of the funniest incidents had to do with a little money we stuck in an envelope with a note, "Buy yourselves a steak with this!" We called them the night after they received the money to see if they had enjoyed the steak and we had to laugh at what had happened. Tom and Patty said: "Thanks for the money you stuck in the letter. We had something other than hamburger for the first time in two weeks, and you know what happened? Tom got the charcoal ready to barbecue the steak (they had spent $2.50 to buy a chuck steak for a family of five) and he put it on, turned away for a minute and their German Shepherd dog (he was probably hungry too) reached up onto the barbecue grill and grabbed the steak and made off with it."

Tom came back on the telephone and said, "I took out after him, and for a moment I was so hungry I forgot I was a Christian, and I said one "little" swear word, apologized immediately to God, and caught the dog and the steak. We were so hungry for something to eat I think if Shezam (the dog) had eaten the steak I would have cut him open to get it back."

The exciting thing to both Charles and me was the fact that in the face of losing a steak when they were so hungry for one, when Tom's carnal nature returned and a "little" swear word came out, he stopped short and apologized IMMEDIATELY to God, before he continued on. We were excited because we saw God moving in small ways in his life. More important, we saw him " wanting" to be what God called him to be.

July 19, 1972 we talked to Tom and Patty and one of the things Tom said was that he was praying that God would make him "want" to obey Him. The greatest secret in the whole Bible is to "want" to obey God and Tom discovered it so soon. We prayed that night, "God, we ask you to give him a double portion of 'wanting to obey you'." . . . but still there was no victory.

In September we received a letter from Patty which said a lot, even though it was a short letter.

"PRAISE THE LORD! Thank you so much for our birthday presents. We were down to about $1.50. After we paid the house payment and the meat payments and gave the Lord 10%, we still had about the same amount left, but what a relief! W-O-W!!!!

Tom and I are getting along about 10,000% better. I think basic insecurities make us feel rejected and we take it out by getting angry. So now we're just working at turning it ALL over to the Lord and letting Him work it out.

We made so many new friends at church—we prayed for Christian fellowship and now we're practically social butterflies. We're going out on the bus tonight to share. We went last week, too. Linda and Larry have been a real blessing to us.

We love you and are anxious to see you. Will you be here in December?

Much love,

Tom, Patty, Wayne, Kim and Edward

My family is going to start coming to church. P.T.L."

We were excited about what that letter said! They had even tithed from their birthday money! Hallelujah, they were learning. They had paid their bills instead of buying something *they* wanted! God was getting through to them. They were getting along better! Praise God, they were beginning to let Him work in their lives. They'd discovered the value of Christian fellowship, and Patty was concerned for her family. We were excited!

We thought about Christmas. This would be the first year our entire family would be celebrating as born again Christians. When the Lord impressed upon us to bring Tom and his family to Houston for a real "JESUS" Christmas, it didn't take much persuading. We planned all kinds of exciting things. No sightseeing, just things designed to show them that you could walk moment by moment with Jesus and have the most exciting life in the world.

The devil heard about it! He didn't like the idea one bit, so he really attacked. Charles and I came back from our last tour before Christmas, and both went to bed with the flu, whacked down harder than we had ever been. The devil was determined we weren't going to have a JESUS Christmas! We didn't even have time to shop before they arrived. We were too busy praying that we'd be out of bed! They drove right straight through from Miami and arrived about 7:30 AM on December 22nd. The excitement was contagious. We knew great things were going to happen, especially after Tom's breakfast prayer.

We discovered the devil had heard the same prayer, and so he redoubled his forces! We all went to our exciting church on Sunday morning. Guess what happened! Tom and Patty ended up warring with each other. We never did find out why. Patty refused to go to church Christmas Eve. Satan was really laughing about this time, I'm sure. Tom went with us to church, but he was so torn up, I'm sure he didn't hear much of the sermon. They asked for a show of hands at the end of those who needed to know Christ. Then a show of hands for those who wanted prayer. Tom misunderstood this and thought that anybody who needed prayer should raise their hand. He put his hand up (unseen by either Charles or me). One of the elders in our church saw Tom raise his hand, and when he didn't come to the altar, he made his way down to him after the service to ask him if he could pray with him. He didn't know who Tom was, but Tom thought we had put him up to it. He said he was really disturbed over their marriage. They had had such high hopes after they accepted Christ that everything was going to work out, but it didn't seem that either of them had the power to keep their marriage on an even keel.

Now it was Christmas Eve. We had somehow managed to get out on Saturday to buy things for the kids. The house was festive looking with lots of presents under the tree. Patty was in the bedroom when we came home, and wouldn't even come out. Not only that, she wouldn't speak to any of us! The devil can really create misery when he wants to.

All of a sudden I realized the devil was trying to win the whole week! I marched into the bedroom, praying all the while that I wouldn't be a typical mother-in-law. I said, "Jesus, let her see the love of God in and through me." I told her she could either ruin the entire week for all of us, or she could grow up and be the kind of a woman God wanted her to be. Praise God, His love must have done it, because she got out of bed and came in with the children so we could all open presents. The atmosphere was still charged with electricity and not the atmosphere of love that it should have been, but things were improving! God allowed this for a beautiful reason, I'm sure, to show them how one person who lets the devil control them can ruin the entire household. We made it through Christmas Eve and the kids had fun.

The week started off with the atmosphere between Tom and Patty cleared up slightly, and then the devil really attacked! In a different way this time though. The baby started running a fever of 104°. We prayed, prayed, prayed and the more we prayed the higher his fever got. They had almost lost him just a few weeks prior to that because of a sensitivity to drugs, so we made a conference call to Miami to a pediatrician there. Can't you imagine the fun the devil was having? With a sick baby, it was hard to spend time reading the Bible, meditating on God's Word. We just plain concentrated on praying that little David would get well.

Then Tom got sick! Next Charles was attacked by another virus, so the house was in an uproar with everyone running a temperature. The devil was really having fun!

Did you ever try to have a Jesus week with everybody getting sick? Did you ever try to have devotions with a sick baby who gets so wound up on medication that he doesn't go to sleep until 2 o'clock in the morning? Did you ever try to read the Bible out loud when everyone has such a sore throat they can't even speak, let alone read? And did you ever try to maintain sprituality 24 hours a day when the devil was attacking from every corner? I believe the Lord allowed this to happen to teach Charles and me that you have a few more problems when you have young children than when your meditation periods are alone without interruption of little children and sickness, and hurt fingers and legs.

We kept praising the Lord. As we came down sick, one by one, we keep praising the Lord more and more. We thanked Him for the flu, for the sore throats, for the virus, for the medication which wound the baby up; we thanked Him for everything that was trying to hinder the Jesus week.

We had accepted a church date between the holidays feeling it would be an exciting service for Tom and Patty to share. Somehow or other, it was not one of those nights of great anointing, and it was a big disappointment to us. Not only that, this was the night Charles got seriously ill.

We kept praising the Lord! We had planned a prayer meeting at our home. By this time I guess we had all rebuked the devil so much he began to let go of us slightly (or was it the praises to God) because we had a wonderful night. The house was jammed to capacity, several people shared their testimonies, we sang in the Spirit, prayed for the sick! The power of the Lord was so beautiful and so present, you couldn't help but be touched. When we asked for those who had come for the baptism, Tom disappeared. I took the women who wanted to receive into our bedroom, and as I turned around, there was Patty saying, "I want to receive the power to make our marriage work!" . . . and the Lord met her in a beautiful way. I didn't want to lay hands on her, because I didn't know how her feelings would be for her mother-in-law to minister to her, so I asked someone else to. Then the Lord said, "I want you to lay hands on her!" I had already ministered to two or three other women, so I simply went over to her and said, "Patty, would you like for me to lay hands on you?" She said, "Yes!" I laid hands on her and asked Jesus to baptize her with the Holy Spirit. He met her so beautifully it exploded all of us in the room. Something happened to Patty in that glorious moment.

As soon as we had finished ministering to the rest of the women, we all sang in the Spirit! What a time we had! Then we went out to the living room to see how Charles was doing, and what Tom was doing. Tom had really kept himself away from all this "emotional" stuff. As soon as he heard that Patty had received, however, he said, "Let me hear you!" (Exactly what Charles had said to me.) Patty prayed in the Spirit for him, and the effect was dramatic! It really turned him on!!! He asked her several times before we all went to bed to pray again and he was fascinated. I think he thought she was the only person in the whole world who could pray in the Spirit.

Patty changed from that moment on! All of a sudden, the new and beautiful Patty began to emerge. Not a defeated Patty, but a Patty who had power to live the Christian life. A Patty who couldn't understand it, but a Patty who now had an extra reserve to draw upon.

The devil had begun to run so fast by this time that we all recovered. New Year's Eve came and we were excited about our Party for the Lord at our church.

An interesting event happened on the way. Our 7 year-old grandson had been so interested in the baptism, he had "eavesdropped" on our conversations all week long, and on New Year's Eve in the car on the freeway, going 60 miles an hour (just like this grandpa), Wayne received the Holy Spirit. Little children who love Jesus receive so freely because they have no hang-ups or barriers in their beliefs. He says he prays his "different" prayers every night! Hallelujah!

Tom again prayed that he would get turned on, but he was reluctant to ask for the baptism. He was afraid that he wasn't good enough, or mature enough, or that he "just wouldn't receive." We couldn't convince him that it isn't anything you work for, it isn't anything you're "good" enough to receive—it's just a beautiful free gift which God gave Jesus the authority to send to the earth, to give us power to live the Christian life. He kept watching Patty, but he was afraid to ask for himself.

The week was over, and they went home! Patty was so excited about what had happened to her, and it became so obvious to other people that something had happened, they began asking her what it was. The first one she began talking to about this new experience was my best friend in Miami. After two days of sharing what this new dimension was all about, and sharing George Otis' tape of HOW TO RECEIVE THE GIFT OF THE HOLY SPIRIT and sharing his book "YOU SHALL RECEIVE . . ." this friend felt she couldn't stand it another minute if she didn't receive, so she asked Tom and Patty down for dinner. It's beautiful how God honors the sincere heart, even when we don't know what we're doing. Patty and my friend went into the bedroom for privacy, and as Patty laid hands on my friend, she was slain in the power and came up speaking in tongues. Hallelujah!!!!! Neither of them knew what had happened, so Daria said, "Why did you push me over?" and Patty, stunned, said, "I didn't push you over—I had only one hand on you and the other up in the air." But now there were two. And both of them were really turned on, and filled with new power.

By "coincidence" several of my charismatic friends in Miami "happened" to go over to Tom and Patty's house the next week. Along with them was the friend who had just received the baptism. As they sat around the dining room table, they all felt impressed to pray particularly for one person, and the Lord had told each one of them the same thing— "TOM." They all laid hands on Tom and Daria prayed and asked Jesus to baptize him. Tom said he had never felt so "clean" in his whole life. He said he felt he had been bathed all over and he tingled for hours. He didn't speak in tongues, but he knew that something had happened to him.

We called Sunday night after we had returned from a trip. Tom began telling us what had happened during the week. He said he was so thrilled about what had happened to Patty they were going to have a meeting the next week because some people wanted to receive whatever it was that Patty had. Both Charles and I said, "You can't expect to give people something you don't even have yourself," and we began talking to him about the power he could expect from the Holy Spirit. He still held back, fear in his heart that he wasn't going to receive, and the knowledge that he would be embarrassed if he didn't. Charles reminded him it was just a question of accepting—no struggling, or anything else. There was such a hungering in Tom's heart, and yet the devil still had his last claw in Tom and was fighting to keep it there.

"Let's all pray in the Spirit together—Frances and I at this end, and you and Patty at that end, Tom, and then you won't feel self conscious" Charles said. We asked Jesus to really baptize Tom. We encouraged Tom to open his mouth and begin praising God but not in English. We knew the words were there! We all prayed in the Spirit, and I could hear Patty's voice,

Charles' voice, and mine, but not a sound out of Tom. The power over the telephone wire was unbelievable! Finally I said, "Tom, I didn't hear anything from you, did I?" He said, "Nope, I had my hand over the receiver." Charles immediately said, "Were you praying in the Spirit?" Tom said, "No, I just had some funny sounds!" Charles said, "Let's hear them—what did they sound like?" Tom gave a few little sounds slowly, and Charles said, "You're praying in the Spirit, son, that's what you're doing." Tom said, "I've had these funny sounding words since Friday night when they laid hands on me; is that what this is?" Charles said, "That's the Holy Spirit within you wanting to pray to the Father in heaven for you!" That must have turned Tom on, because all of a sudden like a mighty, rushing river, came tumbling out of him the most beautiful powerful language you ever heard. He was so excited he drowned out the rest of us as his spirit soared to the Father in heaven; "For one who speaks in a tongue speaks not to men but to God; for no one understands him, but he utters mysteries in the Spirit." The Holy Spirit had come to reside in Tom the rebel, and to give him the POWER he needed to live the Christian life.

As soon as he finished praying in the Spirit, Charles prayed and thanked Jesus for baptizing him in such a beautiful and positive way. The minute Charles finished, we heard Tom's voice on the other end. Momentarily both Charles and I thought he was talking to us. Then we realized it was his soul again crying out to God and the words I heard brought a flood of Holy Spirit tears into my life as I heard a prayer I had waited for so long: "Father," he pleaded, "take out of me *everything* that still wants to sin. Everything, everything, everything!!!! Up until this time there had been no power to pray this way, but now he was pleading with God to crucify the "old nature" to rid him of the carnal desire that was still there to sin.

84

What a night!!!!! Charles and I both cried and praised God and thanked God for what He had done that very night. We praised Him that Tom and Patty were now both baptized with the Holy Spirit, and we rejoiced, rejoiced, rejoiced! We sure didn't get much sleep because of the Holy Spirit excitement that just permeated our being!

Then came Thursday night and we were getting ready to leave on a tour, and called to see how things were going. They had some friends at their house who had come over to discover more about the Holy Spirit, and Tom asked us an interesting question. He KNEW something had happened to him; he KNEW whatever it was it ought to be shared with everyone; he KNEW it was of God, but he honestly didn't know what he knew, so he said, "Look, this guy's got everything, he's got a good job, he's got money, he and his wife don't have any problems, how can I 'sell' him on the Holy Spirit? Why does he need Him?" Both Charles and I had to laugh. All we had to do was to think back a few short weeks and it was hard to believe this was the same Tom. And here he was so excited about something he didn't really know much about, but something he knew had turned him on. We told him it's a command of Jesus, and gave him Ephesians 5:18 "And be not drunk with wine, wherein is excess; but be filled with the Spirit." Jesus commanded us to be filled with the Spirit, and what better reason do we need than that?

Later on that night (about 1 AM) they just had to call us back. Tom said, "Patty really has a gift of ministering the baptism, because our friend received tonight!" We praised the Lord for this, and we said to Tom, "what did you tell her husband?" Tom quoted the verse we had given him, and the husband said, "Well, I'm sort of a Sunday morning Christian. I go to church on Sunday morning, but the rest of the week, I sorta do my own thing, and I'll have to get some things straightened out before I can ask for the baptism. I'll really have to make a commitment."

Tom's advice thrilled us all the way down to our toes as he said, "Do you know the song JUST AS I AM? That's the way God wants you—just as you are so He can do the work. He doesn't want you to do a thing except be willing." Then Tom continued, "As a matter of fact, the baptism is what enabled me to make a total commitment to Jesus!" My cup overflowed with joy. Jesus had promised me that He had come, that my cup would overflow with joy, and it really did to hear my rebel son say the baptism was the thing that gave him the power to make the commitment he had wanted to make for so long. Up until that time, he had tried to make the commitment on his own, but this time the resurrection power of Jesus Christ had surged through him as the Holy Spirit gave him the desire and power to commit his life to Christ. Hallelujah!

Chapter 6

WATCH OUT —
HERE COME THE
LITTLE DEVILS!!!

Life has been one exciting bombshell after another since we received the baptism with the Holy Spirit. We have been eager and open for everything God has for us, but we had reservations about the real activity of demons. We had seen people become so preoccupied with binding Satan and casting out demons they had no time left over to praise God, love Him, or serve Him. We sure didn't want to fall into that trap! We've seen people get so hung up on this subject they visualize demons on every door knob. Every person they meet seems to be loaded with demons and some lose their perspective completely where this subject is concerned. You can also go the other direction, too, and lose your perspective and fail to realize that demons do exist!

Did you ever stop to think how much time Jesus spent casting out demons? In the excellent book on the subject, DELIVER US FROM EVIL, Don Basham emphasizes the fact that "one-fourth of Christ's public ministry dealt with deliverance, a full quarter that almost totally, incomprehensibly, has been left out of the Church's life for years and years—censored." We began to wonder more and more if there was any way a Spirit-filled Christian could continue to ignore this subject, and as always, God showed us in His perfect way, that we had to learn how to stand against demons.

Every time the subject of demonology came up, we'd say, "Let Derek Prince or Don Basham do it, we like what God's called us for," but because of so many little things that happened (?) we began to wonder if anyone could afford to be without the knowledge of what to do with a demon, because sooner or later, if you're out on the battlefield of the Lord, you're going to run right smack into one. And we guarantee you you'll run into them in such a way you won't be able to ignore them.

We had a good reason to shy away from demons. Look what happened to Charles shortly after he committed his life a few years ago and was earnestly seeking how God wanted to use him.

I knew God had put a special call for service on my life. He had already told me to reduce my C.P.A. professional time to one half, but I didn't know what He wanted me to do. Through a series of circumstances which I felt God was bringing about, I decided he might be saying "demonology." I had heard a little about this and didn't like the idea, but I was willing to do anything for God whether I liked it or not.

I had heard a minister say one time that if you ever cast out a demon, you should have several strong men around because they come out fighting. He was relating an actual encounter in his life. What I have found out since is that it is the power of the Holy Spirit and the authority of Jesus which delivers a person from demons. Without the baptism with the Holy Spirit, it is dangerous to encounter demons, or to try to rob Satan's kingdom.

I ordered several books about demons and they (the books, not the demons) arrived one Saturday. I glanced through them. When I got home from church Sunday, I said, "God, I'm going to spend all afternoon really going into the subject so I ask you to reveal all I'm to know and store it into my mind." It was a beautiful, sunshiny day; church had been exhilarating, I was happy and anxious to get started. Everything seemed perfect and I was feeling great!

I started reading, looking up Scriptures and moving studiously into what I felt might be my assigned function in God's kingdom on earth. About thirty minutes passed when suddenly a deep, dark depression came over me. I felt like the whole world caved in and a thousand pound dark cloud came over me. I quickly laid the book on the sofa, stepped into my bedroom and dropped to my knees. I silently screamed to God, and said, "Father, if this is Satan, get him away from me and draw close to me!" The Holy Spirit had stored in my mind for just such a need James 4:7. "So give yourselves humbly to God (and I had). Resist the devil and he will flee from you. And when you draw close to God, God will draw close to you." Instantly, with no lapse of time, the depression lifted, I felt like the sun suddenly burst out of a dark cloud, my head felt free, and a spirit of joy and peace came into me. Are Satan's spirits real? I can assure you they are and he had sent a real live spirit of depression to destroy me. The Holy Spirit had the answer waiting when Satan attacked. I can't stress enough to Christians the importance of daily meditating upon Scriptures.

I put the books on demons way in the back of my bookshelves and never expected to read them again. I felt God had said loud and clear to stay away from the area of demonology! I'm sure He just wanted to prepare me for when He was ready for me to face a spirit world unfamiliar to me then. "For we are not fighting against people made of flesh and blood, but against persons without bodies—the evil rulers of the unseen world, those mighty satanic beings and great evil princes of darkness who rule this world; and against huge numbers of wicked spirits in the spirit world." (Eph. 6:12)

Go back two verses (verse 10-11) "Last of all I want to remind you that your strength must come from the Lord's mighty power within you. Put on all of God's armor so that you will be able to stand safe against all strategies and tricks of Satan."

George Otis has beautifully and clearly displayed Satan's many strategies and tricks in his book LIKE A ROARING LION. He has exposed the coy, seemingly innocent ways he creeps, like the silent snake he is, into the lives of people who do not even recognize satanic scenes in the living room of their Christian hearts.

Because of our ignorance of the subject, we both really tried to keep away from anything that had to do with demons, but at a Winning Women Retreat in Kalamazoo, Michigan someone asked us to cast out a demon. We had to be honest and say we didn't know how. A Catholic nun who had had experience in this field was there, and we called on her and the woman was delivered. Neither of us were in on the deliverance, but we were looking in through a window and what we saw we didn't like! We decided right then and there we'd leave the demons up to Derek, Don, and Catholic nuns!

God continued to deal with us on this subject. In Springfield, Missouri the power of God had really been manifested, some dramatic miracles had occurred in the healing ministry, and several people had been slain in the Spirit. Many had accepted Christ and there was a real moving of God's Spirit. At the end of the service, a very attractive young woman came up to Charles and said, "I don't believe in this business of being slain in the Spirit; show me where it's scriptural!" Charles directed her to the 18th chapter of John, verse 6 in the Living Bible. This is where Jesus was in the Garden of Gethsemane, and the soldiers came up to him and he said, "Whom are you looking for?" "Jesus of Nazareth," they replied. "I am he," Jesus said. AND AS HE SAID IT, THEY ALL FELL BACKWARDS TO THE GROUND." She said "I still don't care, that's not scriptural!" Isn't it funny how people get hung up on little details?

Charles asked her what happened to Saul on the road to Damascus? Whose power had knocked Saul down? Only the power of God, nothing else, and God is still doing it today!

I was standing over to one side, and I really began praying because I realized that Charles was up against something different. I hadn't heard the conversation, but I could tell by the look on his face that this was a unique situation.

Charles, in his usual gentle way, continued to speak to her, and all of a sudden I saw him stiffen and I saw the color drain out of his face I knew not to interrupt, but I really increased my prayers. The next thing I knew, I heard Charles say: "Satan, come out of this girl!"

Nothing happened.

Charles repeated it, only a little louder this time: "Satan, come out of this girl!"

Nothing happened.

Charles repeated it much louder this time: "Satan, come out of this girl!"

Still nothing happened. Then my conservative C.P.A. husband who is as gentle and loving and kind as any man in the entire world began to almost yell "Satan, come out of this girl!" He finally began to shake all over. Nothing happened! She continued to stare at him and finally after Charles had almost made himself hoarse, she turned on her heel contemptuously and ran out of the meeting. Outside she lashed out at another man and slapped him.

Charles came over to me and said cold chills had gone up and down his spine when he realized that he was dealing with a real live demon on the inside of a human being. He said as he looked at her, he was aware that the eyes that were looking at him were not the eyes of the woman who was standing in front of him. In back of her eyes were two little beady eyes that looked very much like the eyes of a little monkey. They just stared at him, and didn't even blink. He said the hate in the eyes "behind the eyes" was unbelievable. He said as he continued to repeat the command the little beady eyes kept looking back at him, laughing, laughing, laughing, laughing. The demons were laughing at Charles because they knew that he didn't know how to cut off their source of power.

We came away defeated! We had come up against a real live demon for the first time in our lives, and didn't know what to do. We saw the tortured girl run out of our lives, knowing we didn't know how to deal with the situation. Charles, still visibly shaken from the ordeal, said, "Let's leave that ministry to some-one who knows what they're doing, because I don't like it." We discussed the situation back in our motel room and decided we didn't want any more to do with demons because it was an unpleasant thing, so we just were going to tell people we didn't have that ministry. Then God spoke to Charles in a beautiful way. He said "Charles, think how many people are going to be in hell if you don't learn how to deal with demons!" Charles said he felt like a knife had been stuck right in his heart and he knew that we could no longer ignore demons. He told me what God had said, and we prayed and said, "Yes, Lord! We don't like this ministry, but teach us how to deal with whatever need is brought to us."

About this time it was as if the Holy Spirit focused a floodlight on certain Scriptures. He often does this to instruct and reveal when He is preparing us for a soon-to-happen event. Look at these:

"But if I am casting out demons by the Spirit of God, then the Kingdom of God has arrived among you. One cannot rob Satan's kingdom without first binding Satan. Only then can his demons be cast out." (Matt. 12:28-30)

"And those who believe shall use my authority to cast out demons, and they shall speak new lan-guages." Mark 16:17

We realized from these Scriptures and others that you were not casting out Satan but rather his demons. That's why the one(s) described above just seemed to laugh at Charles. We realized that all miracles of healing and of people falling under the power, etc. were by the power of God, directed to the person's need by Jesus. Then we realized that Satan's power was in a like manner available to his servants—his spirits or demons. We were acutely aware of what would happen if we were cut off from God's power—we would be helpless. Now we realized that if Satan's power is cut off from his servants, they are helpless. Now read Matt. 12:28-30 again (above).

Something else was revealed in Mark 16:17. "They will be able even to handle snakes with safety, and if they drink anything poisonous, it won't hurt them; and they will be able to place their hands on the sick and heal them." Who is the snake, the serpent? All throughout the Bible, Satan is referred to as a snake. (Rev. 20:2 "He seized the dragon—that old SERPENT the devil, Satan . . .") It was evident then that we have the authority of Jesus and the power of the Holy Spirit to handle Satan (the snake) with safety. Notice in Mark 16 that the same authority and power which brings about healing the sick, also is the authority and power which enables believers to cast out demons and speak other languages. It was not until we received the Holy Spirit that these signs followed: Satan was bound, demons were cast out, people were healed and we spoke in other languages.

We have prayed many times for the girl whose identity we don't know. We have prayed that God has sent someone to her who knows how to minister to her needs and we pray at this time that she has peace in her soul, but it was a horrible memory to take with us, knowing that we had failed God because we weren't equipped. We didn't have on the whole armor of God. We went to battle unequipped. We determined we would prepare so this would never happen again.

Our second encounter with a demon came right in our own home! God didn't want us to be able to run from this one. We have fabulous meetings in our home about once a month when we find a night we're going to be in town, and hundreds of people have received the baptism at these meetings. Healings take place, people accept Christ, and people have really gotten turned on for Jesus just by gathering with other exciting Christians. We sing a little, pray a lot, and let the Holy Spirit guide the meetings and things really begin to happen. At one of these meetings we had just finished sharing some of the miracles God had been doing when the doorbell rang. Most people don't ring the doorbell, they just come in on prayer meeting night, but I guess this was to alert everyone there that something was going to happen. There were 123 people in our home that night. We were sitting wall to wall on the floor and those who had brought their own folding chairs were sitting on them and we were really jammed in. A singing group we know was in town. They had brought their P.A. system over and hooked it up and we had a loud speaker in every room in the house. There were two mikes in our foyer, so Charles stood facing one room and I stood facing the other room, as we had jointly shared some fresh manna.

The bell rang, and someone answered it. I looked up and there was a young man we had been alerted to pray for during the last 48 hours. We had prayed and prayed and prayed because it had been feared he was really possessed by demons. We prayed that he would come to our meeting, and there he stood! I took one look at him, and in the fleeting second before I threw my arms around him, I saw those "eyes behind the eyes!" I remembered in a hurry that the man is the spiritual leader of the home and quickly stepped back to let Charles take his authority. He did, and with the microphone still in his hand, he firmly said, "Satan, I bind you!" At that moment, the demon possessed young man shouted, "If there's anyone here who has not been born again, look out, because something horrible is coming out." He looked like a wild man!

Charles continued: "Satan, I bind you, and now that you're bound those demons inside our brother have lost their source of power. In the name of JESUS, by the power of God's Spirit, and with the authority given by Jesus Christ, I command you evil, foul demons to come out of this man!"

I nearly fainted! God had given Charles the knowledge, power and authority and Charles had not weakened but had spoken boldly and with authority to Satan and his demons. We looked at Ted and the anguish in his face would have broken your heart, only it wasn't his face that we saw . . . it was the demon. His mouth opened wider than any mouth we had ever seen, a bloodcurdling scream came out, Ted convulsed as he arched completely backwards and his head almost touched his feet. He fell to the floor, FREE! Immediately Charles began to talk again and gave anyone there the opportunity to pray and receive Christ as their Saviour and Lord! All of this had gone completely throughout the house on the speaker system, and even those in rooms where they could not see the foyer were aware of what was going on. What a way to start a prayer meeting! The electricity that crackled through the air was so powerful we asked those who had come for healing to come forward right then, because we knew that God would hear and healings would be done for His glory. Many people fell under the power of God that night, never to be the same again! And 123 people were convinced that Satan is real and that demons do exist in our world today! And Charles and Frances believe this, too, but praise God we discovered the first thing to do was to bind Satan.

Isn't it really simple? If we operate without the power of the Holy Spirit, we are cut off from our source of power. And when we are cut off from our source of power, we have absolutely no power to enable us to do a single thing, and the same thing is true of Satan's disciples (or demons). Once you bind Satan he has to sit on the sidelines, and the demons have no choice but to come out when ordered to do so. It is similar to an unborn baby. If the umbilical cord inside the mother was cut, there would be no source of life for the baby. And the demons have no source of power when you bind Satan and put him to rout. Hallelujah!

The next time we came face to face with a demon (that we recognized) happened to me on a one day trip where Charles couldn't go with me. I had gone to Dallas just for the day and was ministering to the needs of the women after brunch. The power of God was so strong that many were slain in the Spirit. Many had accepted Christ this day. There were many people there who had never been to any type of charismatic meeting, who were seeing things they had never seen before.

One woman came up and as I asked her what her need was, I looked at the "windows of her soul" and guess what I saw! Those two little evil eyes peering out at me behind her eyes. (And Charles wasn't there to help me!) As soon as I held her hands in mine, she began to shout, "I don't believe this, I don't believe this, I don't believe this." Then a blood curdling scream! I gently touched her and said, "Jesus, bless her," and she floated to the floor, under the power of God. The hate in her eyes was pathetic as she screamed, "I don't believe this, I don't believe this!" Quickly and quietly I said, "Satan I bind you. You are a liar and you have no place here, and now you have no power." Then I spoke to the evil spirit and said, "By the Spirit of God and in the name of Jesus, I command you evil, foul spirit of unbelief to come out of this woman right now, never to return again." A small wail came out, a drawn out mournful sound, and the look in her eyes was the same as a dog that has been hit by an automobile and is about to draw its last breath. The look said, "You've killed me, you've killed me!" And that's what had happened! The demon of unbelief in her had been cast out and consequently its effective power in her destroyed.

She lay under the power of God for probably 30 minutes, and when she came out from under the power, the peace on her face was beautiful to behold. She was FREE, FREE, FREE!

The next woman in line said, "I want to talk to you, and nobody else, because I'm so afraid. I'm so scared." Her voice got louder and louder and there was absolute terror in her voice. Again I looked in her eyes and saw that hated thing—the evil eyes peering out at me. Even though the hair stood up on the back of my neck, I quietly and calmly held her hands and said, "Jesus, touch her!" And down she went! As she went down I said, "Satan, I bind you. Your power over her is gone forever! Then I said, "Spirit of fear, in the name of Jesus and by the Spirit of God, I command you to leave this woman forever, never to return!" She lay on the floor, sobbing! Holy Spirit tears ran freely all over the place. Here was someone who had been afraid of the baptism with the Holy Spirit and anything connected with it, and the Holy Spirit washed her clean. I saw her mother at a meeting a week later and the mother told me the daughter had originally come up for healing, but because of the spirit of fear, had neglected to ask for healing, but the Lord had healed her as the cleansing tears of the Holy Spirit flowed. Isn't God fabulous to take care of our needs before we even say them?

Demons or evil spirits do not all react alike. Just look at this story of a lady who came for prayer as scores were being healed and were falling backwards to the floor under the power. She said she couldn't believe this, but wanted to. There had been, as I recall, a darkness or depression in her life for which she wanted me to pray. I spoke to the spirits of unbelief—and depression, and commanded them to come out in the name of Jesus, thanked Jesus and asked him to bless her. She started falling to the floor. She seemed to be floating backwards as she was going down very slowly. Her body remained perfectly straight and as she was about halfway down she looked at me and said, "WHAT ARE YOU DOING TO ME?" I felt she had just become aware of the tremendous power of God. Shortly after that I read in the fifth chapter of Mark the account of a demon-possessed man who ran out from a graveyard to Jesus and fell down before Him. "Then Jesus spoke to the demon within the man and said, 'Come out, you evil spirit.' It gave a terrible scream, shrieking, 'WHAT ARE YOU GOING TO DO TO ME, JESUS, SON OF THE MOST HIGH GOD? For God's sake, don't torture me!' " Was that the evil spirit in her saying to me, "What are you doing to me?"

After God began His miracle business in our ministry, we prayed for many people who were deaf or hard of hearing. It seemed almost none were healed. One night a young man came to our house for dinner. He told of his experience of many deaf people being healed as he commanded the spirit of deafness to leave. Our ears perked up!!! Shortly after that at our home prayer meeting as people were leaving, we were bidding them goodnight. As a young woman shook hands with me, I said "Jesus didn't meet your need tonight, did he?" When she replied "no" I asked her what it was. She said, "I'm deaf in my left ear." I placed my hand on her ear, and commanded the spirit of deafness to depart. She slumped to the floor as the power of God's Spirit touched her. She immediately stood up and I asked her to close her right ear with her finger. When she did, I asked what she heard. She said, "I hear you talking—I'm healed!" Since then we have seen many deaf healed when the spirit of deafness is commanded (by the authority of Jesus) to leave.

Then we went to Iowa. We had had two sessions and were looking forward to a short rest period before we continued with another session. Someone came to us and said a woman was really having problems and would we go and minister to her. Charles and I left immediately to see what we could do. She was in the parsonage and when we walked in the room she began to scream, "You're fakes. All you do is double talk. You were just sent up here to confuse us. I hate you!" You see, a demon can't stand the presence of the Holy Spirit because they know it's a losing battle, and they're going to fight until the last moment. We walked over to her, and again those little beady eyes were glaring at us. Quietly we said, "Satan we bind you! You've lost your power over this woman." Then in quick succession we said the thoughts which I'm sure were implanted into our minds by God with the word of knowledge: "Spirit of unbelief, come out of this woman. Spirit of fear, come out of this woman. Spirit of confusion, come out of this woman. Spirit of hate, come out of this woman. As she stood up, her body convulsed, and she fell to the floor. The demons had left, and the first words she said to us were, "I really love you. God sent you here!" We put her back in bed and asked Jesus to put a spirit of sleep on her, and before we got to the door she was sound asleep! Peace and quiet now reigned in her soul.

The subject of demons isn't a nice one, is it? But what a demon does to a person isn't nice either, and the demons that Jesus dealt with weren't very nice! I think of the two men who lived in a cemetery and were so dangerous that no one could go through that area, and Jesus sent the demons into the herd of pigs. That wasn't an especially nice scene, was it? And yet it was something that Jesus had to do. (Matthew 8:28-33) Then there is the story over in Luke 8:26-36 of the one man who also lived in a cemetery in the Gerasene Country. "Homeless and naked, he lived in a cemetery among the tombs. As soon as he saw Jesus he shrieked and fell to the ground before him screaming: 'What do you want with me, Jesus, Son of God Most High? Please, I beg you, oh, don't torment me!' For Jesus was already commanding the demon to leave him. This demon had often taken control of the man so that even when shackled with chains he simply broke out and rushed out into the desert, completely under the demon's power. 'What is your name?' Jesus asked the demon. 'Legion,' they replied, for the man was filled with thousands of them! They kept begging him not to order them into the Bottomless Pit. A herd of pigs was feeding on the mountainside nearby, and the demons pled with him to let them enter into the pigs. And Jesus said they could. So they left the man and went into the pigs, and immediately the whole herd rushed down the mountainside and fell over a cliff into the lake below, where they drowned. The herdsmen rushed away to the nearby city, spreading the news as they ran. Soon a crowd came out to see for themselves what happened and saw the man who had been demon-possessed sitting quietly at Jesus' feet, clothed and sane! And the whole crowd was badly frightened. Then those who had seen it happen told how the demon-possessed man had been healed."

Now reread this chapter and see if the same thing isn't happening today as Christians are being courageous enough to bind Satan and cast the demons out. God is still doing the same miracles today he did when Jesus walked the earth, and the multitudes are still frightened, and the end results are still the same! After the demons have been cast out, the person delivered sits quietly at Jesus' feet.

We are still praying that God will enable us to deal with all kinds of demons as we encounter them. We're also still praying just as fervently that He won't ask us to go out looking for the vicious ones. We love the other parts of our ministry much more, but each time we might be tempted to shy away from demons, we remember what God said to Charles, "How many people will be in hell if you don't learn how to deal with demons!"

Lord, we don't want anyone there because we failed you.

Chapter 7

GOD USES ORDINARY HANDS

The "laying on of hands" is mentioned numerous times in both the Old and New Testaments. God has always used hands in accomplishing His divine will and purpose. In consecrating offerings, Leviticus 1:4 says: "The person bringing it is to LAY HIS HANDS upon its head, and it then becomes his substitute:" "The man who brings the animal shall LAY HIS HAND upon its head and kill it at the door of the Tabernacle. (Lev. 3:2)

The "laying on of hands" for the consecration of men for service is also throughout the Bible. "Then bring the Levites to the door of the Tabernacle as all the people watch. There the leaders of the tribes shall LAY THEIR HANDS upon them, and Aaron with a gesture of offering, shall present them to the Lord as a gift from the entire nation of Israel." Numbers 8:9-10 "And the Lord said unto Moses, Take thee Joshua the son of Nun, a man in whom is the spirit, and LAY THINE HAND UPON HIM." (Numbers 27:18) In Acts 6:6 when the believers were multiplying rapidly, they selected seven men, wise and full of the Holy Spirit. "These seven were presented to the apostles, who prayed for them and LAID THEIR HANDS on them in blessing." I Tim. 4:14 says: "Be sure to use the abilities God has given you through his prophets when the elders of the church LAID THEIR HANDS UPON YOUR HEAD." I Tim. 1:6 says:

"This being so, I want to remind you to stir into flame the strength and boldness that is in you, that entered into you when I LAID MY HANDS upon your head and blessed you."

Jesus certainly believed in the laying on of hands. Matt 19:14 says: "But Jesus said, 'Let the little children come to me, and don't prevent them. For of such is the Kingdom of Heaven.' And he PUT HIS HANDS ON THEIR HEADS and blessed them before he left." "A deaf man with a speech impediment was brought to him, and everyone begged Jesus TO LAY HIS HANDS on the man and heal him." (Mark 7:32) ". . . and they will be able to PLACE THEIR HANDS on the sick and heal them." (Mark 16:18) "As the sun went down that evening, all the villagers who had any sick people in their homes, no matter what their diseases were, brought them to Jesus, and the TOUCH OF HIS HANDS healed every one!" (Luke 4:40) "One Sabbath as he was teaching in a synagogue, he saw a seriously handicapped woman who had been bent double for eighteen years and was unable to straighten herself. Calling her over to him Jesus said, 'Woman, you are healed of your sickness!'" HE TOUCHED HER, and instantly she could stand straight. How she praised and thanked God!" (Luke 13:10-13) "Paul went in and prayed for him and LAYING HIS HANDS ON HIM, healed him! Then all the other sick people in the island came and were cured." (Acts 8:8) "Large crowds followed Jesus as he came down the hillside. Look! A leper i approaching. He kneels before him, worshippin,. 'Sir,' the leper pleads, 'if you want to, you can heal me.' Jesus TOUCHES THE MAN. 'I want to' he says: 'be healed.' And instantly the leprosy disappears." (Matt. 8:3) "When Jesus arrived at Peter's house, Peter's mother-in-law was in bed with a high fever. BUT WHEN JESUS TOUCHED HER HAND, the fever left her; and she got up and prepared a meal for them!" (Matt. 8:14-15) "They went right into the house where he was staying and Jesus asked them, 'Do you believe I can make you see?' 'Yes, Lord,' they told him, 'we do.' Then HE TOUCHED THEIR EYES and said, 'Because of your faith it will happen.' " (Matt. 9:28-29)

Jesus used his hands to calm his disciples, too. "At this the disciples fell face downward to the ground, terribly frightened. Jesus came over and TOUCHED THEM. 'Get up,' he said, 'don't be afraid.' " (Matt. 17:1) He used his hands for many purposes.

"And God wrought special miracles by the HANDS of Paul: so that from his body were brought unto the sick handkerchiefs or aprons, and the diseases departed from them, and the evil spirits went out of them." (Acts 19:11) Just the hands of Paul on material brought healing to the sick!

Something special is communicated by the hands, even the hands of those who touched Jesus. "Wherever he went—in villages and cities, and out on the farms— they laid the sick in the market places and streets, and begged him to let them at least TOUCH the fringes of his clothes; and AS MANY AS TOUCHED HIM WERE HEALED." (Mark 6:56) "Everyone was trying to TOUCH him, for when they did, healing power went out from him and they were cured." (Luke 6:19) "Who touched me?" Jesus asked. Everyone denied it, and Peter said, "Master, so many are crowding against you . . ." But Jesus told him, "No, it was someone who deliberately TOUCHED ME, for I FELT HEALING POWER GO OUT FROM ME." (Luke 8:45-46)

Not only were hands used for healings and blessings, the Bible records laying on of hands for the baptism with the Holy Spirit. "Then Peter and John LAID THEIR HANDS upon these believers, and they received the Holy Spirit." (Acts 8:17) "Then, when Paul laid his HANDS upon their heads, the Holy Spirit came on them, and they spoke in other languages and prophesied." (Acts 19:6)

An exciting laying on of hands was done by Ananias who laid hands on Saul. Immediately it was as though scales fell from his eyes and he was healed. Ananias was not a well known character in the Bible, and yet the simple laying on of hands healed the man who was to become one of the greatest disciples of all times. God uses the hands of ordinary people today, too!

When Jesus passes by a lot of things can happen in a hurry. We love to see people who are ready for spiritual "open heart" surgery by the Lord because He can really do miracles in their lives then. Let's look at a few miracle stories as Jesus passed by and touched them. This man met Jesus in less than five minutes as Saviour, Baptizer and Healer!

"While attending a Baptist church in Fort Worth, Texas, at the age of 17, I had my first meaningful encounter with the Lord Jesus Christ. For the next 45 years I lived in denominational bliss, my old sin nature was in high gear, racing down the broad highway of self-righteousness, but with the Lord's 'hook' in my jaw. On April 8, 1972, my Lord Jesus Christ reeled me in—I met him as Saviour and Lord!

In November, 1969, the Lord let me feel the first tug on the 'hook' in my jaw, to get my attention. A continuous bleeding, without pain, started from my bladder. A doctor in Stanford, Conn. advised me I had a cancer of the bladder, Grade I, Malignant. An operation stopped the bleeding and I was advised to return every 90 days to check progress. I did not go back because I knew I was healed as I had trusted the doctor's skill for the healing.

August, 1970, our company sent us back to Texas and there again the bleeding started with no pain. The Houston doctor advised, after examination, that the cancer had progressed to Grade II, Malignant. Now, after three minor and one major operation with no arrest of the bleeding (still no pain), the doctors advised cobalt treatments, which I declined.

In 1968, my daughter Barbarah had received the baptism of the Holy Spirit and tried to share her experience with me. I assured her I was a satisfied Baptist, but if she wanted to believe that way it was all right.

From February to April, 1972, there was a real spiritual warfare at the 'Henry Hilton' (our year around beach home). On the top side was the Lord saying "Come unto me, The Great Physician, I'll show you the meaningful way.' On the bottom side there was the enemy telling me to destroy myself. One spirit would say, 'Use the 25 mm pistol,' another would say, 'Use trichloroethylene in a coke,' and the third said, 'Run your boat into the Gulf of Mexico with 28 gallons of gasoline and fall out accidentally.' The Lord kept saying, 'Come unto me, The Great Physician, I'll show you the meaningful way.' Then those evil ones said to me, 'Use me, be sure.'

Barbarah tried to reach someone with the Full Gospel Businessmen's Fellowship International to help me. She couldn't locate anyone. Later, a friend showed me an article on Captain John LeVrier of the Houston Police Department, who had had a miracle healing of a like cancer through Kathryn Kuhlman's ministry in California. (See Kathryn Kuhlman's book CAPTAIN LEVRIER BELIEVES IN MIRACLES.) I called the Captain to verify the story. (I was a real doubter—like Thomas). He stated it was completely true, and suggested I go to a regional meeting of the Full Gospel Businessmen.

On April 7, the first day, I heard testimonies of lay people like myself that made me know something was happening in me. That night we went home and my sweet wife examined my blood saturated pants and said, 'You are bleeding too much to go back tomorrow.' I said, 'I like what I heard and I have never seen such love in people in my life. I am going to bathe, sleep and be back at 7:30 A.M..'

The next morning, Capt. LeVrier said, 'Stoney, here is someone I want you to meet!'—Praise the Lord!

He introduced me to Charles and Frances Hunter and their daughter Joan. Charles said, 'The Lord told me anyone wanting the baptism of the Holy Spirit should come to this side of the room and anyone wanting healing should go to the other side of the room. Which do you want first?' I could only blubber, 'Both.'

Frances asked me point blank: 'Are you saved?' I could only answer, 'I'm not sure!' She said, 'Pray this prayer after me, and you'll KNOW you're saved!' And so she led me through the sinner's prayer and all of a sudden I knew that I knew that I knew I was SAVED! Hallelujah! Then Charles and Frances laid hands on me and Frances prayed for Jesus to baptize me with the Holy Spirit. Rivers of tears flowed as a new language came forth. Then Charles prayed and asked Jesus to heal me. He rebuked the spirit of cancer in Jesus' name, and then I heard Charles, after a big bear hug say, 'Stoney, claim your healing in the name of Jesus.'

Can you imagine all this in a split second? Saved, baptized with the Holy Spirit and healed! I went to the rest room and my preparation for bleeding was found with not a drop of blood. Hallelujah! Praise the Lord!

I have since been to M.D. Anderson Hospital on two successive 90 day periods and they can find no need for treatment. Praise the Lord. I have not had a cobalt treatment and by faith, I know His word is true. He said, 'By my stripes you were healed.' I AM. Praise the Lord.

(signed) C.L. "Stoney" Henry"

A woman had bleeding ulcers so bad she could not sleep much at night. We were at a retreat, and during prayer time I barely tapped her stomach (because that was what God indicated that I do) and asked her to take a deep breath and say, "Praise the Lord!" The next morning at breakfast she came to us and said when my finger touched her, it was like a thousand electric needles went through her as Jesus made her whole.

106

Another lady came to us in the cafeteria at the same retreat and said she had calcium deposits on her neck which had steadily become worse over the past five years. Her doctor could do little to help. Her neck was stiff and she could turn it just slightly. While she was talking I touched the back of her neck and softly said, "Jesus, touch her!" I asked her to turn her head. She looked puzzled, but followed the instruction and was instantly and totally healed!

Even "little" miracles are BIG if you're the person involved!

A boy about ten years of age came to me in a miracle service and when asked what his need was, he said, "I have cramps in my stomach." Quickly I lightly tapped his stomach and said, "Jesus, touch him." Then I asked him to take a deep breath and say, "Thank you, Jesus," which he did. I asked him, "Where is the pain?" What a look of surprise and joy as he said, "It's gone!"

In a miracle service in a Presbyterian Church in Youngstown, Ohio, a boy about 10-12 years of age came to me on crutches. I asked what happened and he and his dad informed me that he had a disease in his right leg which the doctor could not diagnose. It had become so bad that he could not stand on it, but had to bear all the right leg weight on his crutch. I touched the leg and said, "Jesus, touch him," and then said, "Let me have your crutches." He unhesitatingly handed them to me, and when I said, "In the name of Jesus, WALK!" He did!!! He walked all over the church altar area, up and down steps and through the sanctuary.

KM from Lubbock, Texas writes: "I had a pinched nerve in my right hip. The doctor called it a segmentation pain. He said I'd have it forever if I exercised much. It began to hurt so badly that I couldn't walk. Then Charles prayed for me and I was healed instantly!"

Mrs. HGB from Michigan writes of relief after 30 years of pain:

"I have had colon trouble thirty years. I took medicine four times a day. I stopped taking the medicine Saturday night when I came up to be healed and Charles prayed that Jesus would heal me. I haven't needed it since. Praise the Lord. This was my first experience of seeing people healed and also of being healed.

"I just want you to know that every morning when I awake the first thought that comes to my mind is, 'I am healed. Praise the Lord!'"

Oh, what a difference since Jesus passed by!

D & L.W. (Nazarene Church) wrote:

"You may not remember us but we met you at the Assembly of God Church on March 27, 1973. It was here that my wife and I and our two children received the baptism of the Holy Spirit and were slain in the Spirit. P.T.L. Our lives have never been the same since that night. Less than a year ago we were getting a divorce, but that night our marriage was healed and we found what we had searched for all our lives! The power of the Holy Spirit came with the new prayer language and all. The next time we saw you was May 8th and we asked you to anoint us and our children for the ministry and all four of us were slain in the Spirit at the same time while we held hands. P.T.L."

This is one of many letters which have shared how God has put marriages back together when we simply laid hands on them and they went under the power together. He does supernaturally in a few seconds what it would take a psychologist years to do, and does a much better job.

From M.M. in Arizona, we received the following letter:

"We started reading your books about four months ago—we just absorbed every one we could get. Then in late March I wrote you a letter thanking you for all we had received from the books. You very graciously sent me the book THE TWO SIDES OF A COIN, which I immediately started reading. (Oh how the Lord works!) Having grown up the daughter of a

Southern Baptist preacher, you can just imagine the hang-ups I had. But through that book, each hang-up was discarded. I shared the book with my friend, and she was absolutely open and had no reservations at all. But we just were not ready at that time I guess. We prayed, but nothing happened.

As we look back over the last four months, it seems to us that the Lord had just plainly been pushing and shoving us ahead to prepare us for May 4, 1973—what a night!

We heard you were coming to town and decided to go. All that day, both of us had horrible days. Satan was throwing every road block he could in our way—and the more he got in the way the more determined we were to go because we knew there must really be a reason he didn't want us there.

That evening—praise the Lord—we were both slain in the Spirit and both of us received the baptism of the Holy Spirit. That was not quite a week ago, and it would take four pages to tell you what God is doing now through us. We feel the Lord meant for this to happen to us at the same time because we now have the fellowship with each other in the Spirit. But it doesn't stop there. We have a prayer circle that started on April 6th with four people. Last night 13 people attended! We have had many wonderful answers to prayer but we can hardly wait to see what will happen now! We feel the Lord will use us to reach others in this group and with that nucleus we will turn our little Methodist church upside-down. (We are going up Saturday evening and anoint all the pews and the pulpit—praise the Lord—I can hardly wait for Sunday!)

We thank you for coming to Arizona and for sharing your new life with us. 'He touched me, and now I am no longer the same!' "

B.G. writes from Amarillo, Texas:

"I had a great need from God to help me from being bitter with resentment because my husband smoked so much. I couldn't overcome this resentment as hard as I tried and had prayed and had others pray, but it got worse and worse.

So, the Sunday you were at the Methodist Church I went. I sat praying for release so long and said, "I don't have to go up there—because if Jesus can help me He can do it where I sit." This was the first time I ever saw people slain in the Spirit. That really didn't bother me, but I guess it was pride that kept me back and you had said you all had to leave soon for the plane, so I thought I'll go up and have Mrs. Hunter pray about the problem because I can't keep living with it.

You asked me my name and before I ever got it out fully I was lifted up and felt as a feather floating—I don't think you even had time to touch me, but praise God this resentment left me as I still continued to talk to Jesus about it on the floor. Many more wonderful things have fallen in place since then. Jesus was the only one who knew why I went, so all power and praise to our wonderful Lord.

My husband hasn't quit smoking yet, but praise God I've quit nagging and being resentful. I know the Lord did this, and He will deliver my husband from smoking in His own way."

In Lubbock, Texas we were praying one night—actually for delivery of cigarette habits, when we asked a lady who had come forward with the others if cigarettes were her problem. She calmly said, "No, I'm blind in my left eye; will you pray?" We placed a hand over the eye and asked Jesus to open it. We said, "Now, what do you see?" She hesitated a moment as she gazed at the audience and suddenly shouted, "I can see, I can see!" This was such a thrill because we had prayed for years for the blind. We asked the lady to tell the congregation of the beautiful miracle God had just done. Then God said to tell the people Jesus would touch them for any need in their life—salvation, physical, spiritual, financial, family relationships—just reach up to Jesus and He will meet you with a miracle; "Father, do miracles in the name of Jesus; Jesus, touch them!"

Two or three minutes later a lady came to us and when we asked her what her need was, she said, "None. I, too, was blind in one eye, but now I see!" Jesus had touched her! She, by faith, accepted her gift of healing from Jesus. All by the power of God.

"And behold, there was a man which had his hand withered . . . . Then saith he to the man, 'Stretch forth thine hand.' And he stretched it forth; and it was restored whole, like as the other." Matt. 12:10, 13 (KJV)

In Clovis, New Mexico in a school auditorium a young man came for prayer. He held out his left hand. It was withered and was much smaller than the other hand. We asked him to hold both hands out in front with fully extended arms, palms together. He did this and we asked our Father to do a miracle in the name of Jesus; in the name of Jesus; IN THE NAME OF JESUS!!! As we repeated the name JESUS, the withered hand began to be recreated and unfolded like a flower until in a matter of seconds both hands were alike! Hallelujah!!! Praise Jesus!! Thank you Father!!!

What an awesome spectacle to see the power of God in clear view of your eyes!

We just returned from Claypool, Indiana, where a man excitedly met us and shared a beautiful story with us. His niece had been with us in Toledo, Ohio, where we prayed for the spirit of cancer to leave her. She had seven cancerous nodules on the inside of her neck. She went under the power and there was no unusual sensation. Ten days later she went to the doctor for examination. There was no cancer. No nodules. Nothing except seven tiny little scars! I put them down as "divine scars!!

Sometimes we think of the ways God has used our hands and it's difficult to believe how he can use hands in so many interesting ways! In Cleveland, Ohio, a little girl came up to me and asked me to pray for a "personal problem!" She was probably seven or eight years old. The Lord gave me a word of knowledge so I knew it was bed wetting, so I asked her, "Do you love Jesus?" She said, "Yes, I really do." Then I asked her if she felt that Jesus could cure this problem. She said she KNEW that He could. I just prayed a simple prayer as I put my hand on her little tummy and another hand on the kidney area in the back. All I asked was that He wake her up at the right times and take care of this problem. She immediately went under the power. The next night she came running up to me, forgetting she hadn't told me her problem and said, "I didn't wet the bed last night!" Praise God, even for "little" prayer answers like this. I saw this little girl's parents three months later and they said she had been dry ever since Jesus touched her!

Judy is a beautiful Christian girl who was planning to be married soon. Following a talk at a FGBMFI many people came forward for prayer. The very first one was Judy and her fiance. Judy said that for about four years she had been plagued almost every night with frightening nightmares. This had disturbed her severely and caused great anxiety about her forthcoming marriage. She asked me to pray for this condition. I said, "Judy, let's ask God what causes these nightmares." The beginning of our prayer was, "Father, will you please reveal the cause of the nightmares, in Jesus' name."

I opened my mind to God and dismissed all thoughts of my own and waited for the answer. It came quickly. I said to Judy, "You have either seriously or in fun, played with ouija boards, read horoscopes, studied astrology or the occult, or have attended seances or something of witchcraft, haven't you?" She said, "Yes, *but just for fun!*" I said, "Judy, that's an abomination to God, a horrible sin against Him. Do you realize that you have looked to a source other than God for answers?" Then I placed my hands on her head and began a prayer for deliverance. She asked God to forgive her for even playfully inviting Satan and his demons to assume control of her mind as she infested it with this evil act of looking into the future by satanic means when God has told us not to be concerned about the future but to trust Him to tell us what we are to do; to trust Him to guide our lives.

Then I prayed, "Satan, I bind you by the power of God's Spirit, in the name of Jesus. Spirits of witchcraft and the occult, I command you to come out in the name of Jesus." (Matt. 12:28-30) Just then God's mighty power touched Judy and she started slowly falling backwards until she was lying on the floor "under the power." She was there several minutes before God had completed His cleansing surgery while she was peacefully under God's spiritual anesthetic.

Before writing this story we called Judy, three months after the prayer. We asked her what happened that night. This is the way she described the sensation and results: "A tingling sensation covered me. I felt clean—like I was going through a cleansing process; I felt a newness, so free. I had for all these years had a pressure on my mind with headaches and a stiffness, and suddenly my mind was freed and the pressure and headache left; I felt like a big bond was taken away. I have felt so wonderful since then. I have not had a nightmare, a headache, a pressure or any other problem. I have had many oppportunities to share the story of the deliverance and healing power of God since Jesus touched me. I feel a great need to let others know how easy it is to 'just in fun' invite the enemy to control us." "But when you follow your own wrong inclinations your lives will produce these evil results . . . spiritism (that is, encouraging the activities of demons), . . ." (Gal. 5:19-20)

Judy is now married to a sincere Christian man, the one who stood beside her that wonderful night. What a difference in her life since Jesus passed by! Thank you, Jesus!

Mrs. E.E.S. from Ohio writes:

"Praise the Lord! It was so merciful of our wonderful Lord to allow you folks to be shared with us in the Cleveland area. Such wonderful things happened during that time. The Spirit was so 'alive' and 'at work' it is hard for laymen like myself to 'breathe all this in.'

On Monday evening at the miracle service Frances called out a hypoglycemia (low blood sugar) healing. It was before the miracle service actually started. You both were giving some of your testimony and Frances pointed to the front left of the lectern. I was seated directly left of the stage. No one publicly claimed the healing. I felt a wonderful relaxed feeling come over me and I thought, "Lord, it can be me." I did claim the healing and know that God could and would give more than one healing for an illness at a time. Since I am one of those who is very cautious and have to 'be sure'—I knew that I would definitely know if God had again touched my body and righted an imbalance. I had not been feeling real good for a few weeks. This illness makes one feel very shakey and insecure when the blood is low. Upon awaking in the morning it seems to be the worst since this is the time that the body has not had food for a while. Well, PRAISE THE LORD, I have not had one 'shakey' morning since that glorious service in the Lakewood Methodist Church and I know that God did touch me."

Look how quickly Jesus did a miracle here!

We had just finished speaking in the Great Melodyland Christian Center in Anaheim, California, and were on our way to a classroom where we had been asked to speak briefly to a class on "How to Make Your Marriage Exciting." We had been detained as we counseled with people and were rushing into the room when we met a teenage girl going out. The Spirit directed our eyes to her and we noticed that she was limping badly; one leg was bent and appeared stiff. We said, "What's the problem?" She said, "Oh, the tendons didn't grow right in my leg, and I've always been like this."

We touched her knee and said, "Jesus touch her." We rushed on to our meeting, but we heard exclamations of excitement from her and her friends.

We didn't have time to check back, but two or three months later we were in a meeting where some of the people from the Melodyland Christian Center were attending. We shared the miracle and asked if anyone could confirm the story. Mike Esses, one of the associate pastors there, came to the microphone and said, "I'm her Sunday School teacher. It was an instant and total healing and her leg is normal." Hallelujah! How we praise you, Jesus, for being available on such short notice!!!!!

Two of the most exciting miracles that had happened to date happened to us in the same meeting, approximately four minutes apart! We were in a large Foursquare Church in the midwest. Just prior to leaving, Frances went to a woman in a wheelchair and after praying, just touched her lightly on the head and said, "Jesus, bless her!" As Frances turned to go back to the pulpit, the woman stood up from her wheelchair, the congregation screamed, Frances turned around, ran back to the woman and said, "In the name of Jesus of Nazareth, WALK!" . . . .

And walk she did! Right out of the wheelchair into Frances' arms and all the way across the church. God had promised that some day we'd see someone get out of a wheelchair and walk. We talked to her on the telephone just before finishing this book and she told us she had rheumatoid arthritis for 12 years. Her comment to us when we asked her what caused her to get up from the wheelchair was just beautiful! She was so surprised when we said we had prayed for her because she said, "All I saw was Jesus telling me to get up, and I wasn't about to disobey Him!" Do you know who cried harder than anyone else? We did! Glory!!!

This is a beautiful story of a beautiful little girl!

"Laura Dawn was born with congenital dislocation of both hips. She had closed surgery and was put in a body cast for a year. The doctors said that her hips were supposed to heal as a result of this.

The right hip healed, but the healing in the left hip was slower so that she was put in a night brace Six months later she was taken back to the doctor. He said there was no progress and that the head of the femur was beginning to deteriorate. The doctor put her in a brace to remain until the hip healed. Nothing more had happened. She could 'walk' with difficulty, pain and limping, but had never been able to run." (The above story was told us by the mother of Laura Dawn.)

Then came the day of the miracle service in her home town. Her daddy brought her forward for prayer. Frances prayed for her at the beginning of the service and as she held the four year old in her arms she knew the power of God was going through the little body. A bulky brace covered her left leg as she hobbled around. She did not return to her seat, neither did her daddy or her sister, but they all stayed at the front of the church. Time had run out and we were getting ready to leave the service in the hands of several other people because we had a chartered plane waiting for us at the airport to take us to a commercial plane in another city. Just as we were getting ready to slip out the back door, someone asked Charles to pray for this little girl. Charles was not aware of the fact that Frances had prayed (it wouldn't have made any difference anyway, he would have prayed again) and he prayed a simple prayer saying, "Jesus, make this hip socket perfect."

The expression on the face of Laura Dawn showed a new dawn of faith had hit her. She must have felt the power of God, because when Charles said to her daddy, "Take off the brace," her little hands tore at the top buckle. Her daddy unbuckled the lower ones and when it loosened, she excitedly pushed it off. She was in a large pulpit chair and even before she could get out of the chair, her little legs were running in the air. She scooted out of the chair and hit the floor running as Charles said, "Run in the name of Jesus!"

Have you ever seen a beach bird or a "killdeer" run—their legs go about a "million miles a minute." This is the way her little legs seemed to go as she ran up and down steps, and across the church. Praise God! SHE HAD NEVER RUN IN HER ENTIRE LIFE BEFORE! She ran like someone who had really been set free. Her daddy put her on his shoulder and held the brace up in the air with his other arm. When she got home she went running to her mother and said, "Jesus made my leg all better!"

Her parents took her back to the doctor who suggested the leg brace be put back on, in spite of what seems to be one of God's beautiful miracles. She has had no pain, no discomfort and has "quiet" play time at night without her brace. We believe that Jesus has healed her. Laura Dawn believes that Jesus has healed her. When the doctor suggested replacing the leg brace, Laura said, "Does this mean that Jesus didn't heal me?" Praise God for her mother who said, "No, honey, it doesn't mean that Jesus didn't heal you!"

Pray with us, will you, for the complete recovery of this darling little girl. Pray that Satan will be bound because there's nothing the devil would like better than to steal a healing of this kind.

We just looked at each other's hands. Very ordinary hands. Frances looked at hers and said, "They just look like an 'old lady's hands.' See those funny little brown spots that come as you get older? There's nothing unusual about them!" Charles looked at his and said, "I don't see anything there, do you?" Frances squeezed them and said, "Honey, I love them because they belong to you! The hair on the back of your hands is turning white, and I think it's beautiful! But the thing that makes them so super special is that they're empty and powerless until Jesus puts them on as gloves as He reaches out to touch someone."

117

Chapter 8

THE POWER OF GOD IS AN AWESOME THING!!!

As this age draws closer and closer to its conclusion, we see more and more of God's power and glory being reflected in services. There are always a few who run from the power of God because they are afraid. We began to wonder about this! Why did people run when God was manifesting Himself?

Suddenly, we began to notice something in the Bible. Watch the definite pattern of these Scriptures and see how they reflect exactly the same fear in the hearts of some! Why? ... because the power of God is an awesome thing! We remember one of the first times we ever saw tremendous power demonstrated in one of our services and hundreds fell under the power. As people were under a supernatural anesthetic, our hearts were really pounding and when we came back home we made the following statement: "The power of God is an awesome thing! More than 700 people fell under the power at Sunday night's meeting! Both of us have said this could be frightening if we didn't know that every cell in our bodies belonged to Jesus Christ!"

Man was never created to be able to look upon God. We are just not constituted to see God's power and glory poured out without some reaction. Oftentimes when we see the supernatural work of God, especially for the first time, it creates a fear in our

118

hearts. "So that the priests could not stand to minister because of the cloud, for the glory of the Lord had filled the house of the Lord." (I Kings 8:11 KJV) Praise God we can be affected and be sensitive to the power of God. If you've ever had fear, read these stories in the Bible, looking this time at the effect on those watching, instead of the miracle! Prepare yourself for the things to come as God continues to pour out His Spirit!

Matthew 9:1-7 tells the story of the paralyzed boy brought to Him on a mat. "Jesus told him 'Pick up your stretcher and go on home, for you are healed.' And the boy jumped up and left." Listen to what verse 8 says: "A CHILL OF FEAR SWEPT THROUGH THE CROWD AS THEY SAW THIS HAPPEN RIGHT BEFORE THEIR EYES. HOW THEY PRAISED GOD FOR GIVING SUCH AUTHORITY TO A MAN!" Watch what happens when the power of God is manifested: "But even as he said it, a bright cloud came over them, and a voice from the cloud said, 'This is my beloved Son, and I am wonderfully pleased with him. Obey him.' At this, the disciples fell face downward on the ground, TERRIBLY FRIGHTENED." (Matt. 17:6)

Lord God, we bow low before your feet, because you alone are worthy of our praise, honor, fear and awe!

The story of the woman with the issue of blood is one of the best known healing miracles in the Bible. Notice what the Bible has to say about her reaction to a personal touch from God: " 'Who touched my clothes?' His disciples said to him, 'All this crowd pressing around you, and you ask who touched you?' But he kept on looking around to see who it was who had done it. Then the FRIGHTENED woman, TREMBLING at the realization of what had happened to her, came and fell at his feet and told him what she had done. 'Daughter, your faith has made you well; go in peace, healed of your disease.' " (Mark 5:28-34)

Is there any story in the Bible where Jesus' power is reflected any more vividly than the story of the storm on the lake? "As evening fell, Jesus said to his disciples, 'Let's cross to the other side of the lake.' So they took him just as he was and started out, leaving the crowds behind (though other boats followed). But soon a terrible storm arose. High waves began to break into the boat until it was nearly full of water and about to sink. Jesus was asleep at the back of the boat with his head on a cushion. Frantically they awakened him, shouting, 'Teacher, don't you even care that we are all about to drown?'

Then he rebuked the wind and said to the sea, 'Quiet down!' And the wind fell, and there was a great calm. And he asked them, 'Why were you so fearful? Don't you even yet have confidence in me?' AND THEY WERE FILLED WITH AWE and said among themselves, 'Who is this man, that even the winds and seas obey him?'"

We love the story of Simon and his lack of fish after fishing all night. Read the story this time, though, not thinking about the size of the catch, but of the effect it had upon those present. "When he had finished speaking, he said to Simon, 'Now go out where it is deeper and let down your nets and you will catch a lot of fish.'

'Sir,' Simon replied, 'we worked hard all last night and didn't catch a thing. But if you say so, we'll try again.'

And this time their nets were so full that they began to tear! A shout for help brought their partners in the other boat and soon both boats were filled with fish and on the verge of sinking.

When Simon Peter realized what had happened, he fell to his knees before Jesus and said, 'Oh, sir, please leave us—I'm too much of a sinner for you to have around.' FOR HE WAS AWESTRUCK BY THE SIZE OF THEIR CATCH, as were the others with him, and his partners too—James and John, the sons of Zebedee." They were awestruck because they had seen with their own eyes the supernatural power of God.

Let's take a look at Jesus walking on the water, and even though the disciples realized that He was the answer, they were TERRIFIED!

"That evening his disciples went down to the shore to wait for him. But as darkness fell and Jesus still hadn't come back, they got into the boat and headed out across the lake toward Capernaum. But soon a gale swept down upon them as they rowed, and the sea grew very rough. They were three or four miles out when suddenly they saw Jesus walking toward the boat! They were TERRIFIED, but he called out to them and told them not to be afraid." John 6:16-20

In their hearts they KNEW that their only answer and hope was in Jesus, and yet when they saw Him walking toward the boat they were terrified! The power of God is surely an awesome thing, and no wonder we are terrified even today when we see the supernatural power of God!

Luke 1:11 shows another type of miracle which created fright. "Zacharias was in the sanctuary when suddenly an angel appeared, standing to the right of the altar of incense! Zacharias WAS STARTLED AND TERRIFIED." And yet think of the good news the angel brought, that Zacharias and his wife Elizabeth were to have a son. If an angel appeared right now we might all be startled and terrified, wouldn't we? We know we would be!!!!!

Luke 24:4 says: "They stood there puzzled, trying to think what could have happened to it." (Jesus' body was missing from the tomb). "Suddenly two men appeared before them, clothed in shining robes so bright their eyes were dazzled. THE WOMEN WERE TERRIFIED and bowed low before them." Another supernatural act of God as He sent two angels down to the empty tomb so that Mary Magdalene and several others who were present could be advised in a heavenly way of what had happened

121

to the body of Jesus. Hallelujah! How would we feel if the same thing happened to us? Exactly the same way, we're sure!

Luke 2:9-11 again deals with a supernatural manifestation. "Suddenly an angel appeared among them, and the landscape shone bright with the glory of the Lord. THEY WERE BADLY FRIGHTENED, but the angel reassured them.

"Don't be afraid!" he said. "I bring you the most joyful news ever announced, and it is for everyone! The Savior—yes, the Messiah, the Lord—has been born tonight in Bethlehem!"

God was letting the world know by the brilliance of His glory that they were about to hear the most joyful news ever, and they were awed and frightened by His mighty power.

Let's look at what the Bible says about Moses: "Forty years later, in the desert near Mount Sinai, an angel appeared to him in a flame of fire in a bush. Moses saw it and wondered what it was, and as he ran to see, the voice of the Lord called out to him, 'I am the God of your ancestors—of Abraham, Isaac and Jacob.' Moses SHOOK WITH TERROR and dared not look." Acts 7:30-32.

Praise God His Word gives us comfort knowing that even the great saints in the Bible shook with terror at the presence of God. But again, let's really praise God that He is pouring out His Spirit in such unlimited quantities. We're ready for all that God has, are you?

We're going to share with you on the following pages some of the comments of people who have been touched by the power of God, and their various reactions.

Life for Laymen, in Denver, Colorado, has one of the most outstanding Bible teachers we've ever heard. Marilyn Hickey, wife of Wally Hickey, pastor of THE HAPPY CHURCH, gives a 10 minute teaching session every Sunday morning on T.V. which would convict even the most hardhearted sinner. Her Bible studies and retreats have grown at a fantastic rate as people flock to her anointed teaching sessions. We recently visited there, made some T.V. tapes, spoke at several luncheons, and then went to the Northern Colorado University in Greeley, Colorado. This letter shares some exciting things that happened as seen through the eyes of the Hickeys:

"Wally and I agreed that we had never been in such a service as the one in the ballroom of the Northern Colorado University at Greeley. You know, an hour before the doors were opened people were standing in the lobby singing worshipful choruses. We have been Assembly of God pastors for fifteen years and loved every moment of it, but I have never seen such a sovereign move of God as that night. As you are well aware when you both stepped on the platform and encouraged the people to join in a clap offering to the Lord (instead of for you), it appeared as though a clap of power hit the 1700 people. The first thing I heard was a thud I looked up and to the left I saw a young woman who had fallen on the floor. Within a few moments a Lutheran girl I knew from the Study Retreats was on the floor behind her. Then suddenly all over the ballroom people had fallen out under the power of God. Some were laughing, some were praising, and speaking in tongues, some lay still and when we left at 11:30, there were still a few on the floor under the power of God in this way. *No human touched them.* We are still laughing with the joy of the Lord about those who were to come to the platform and testify of the healings they received and fell under the power as they started up the steps. I have no idea how many married couples came up to rededicate their married life to God and ended up on the floor. I laughed, I cried, I rejoiced and then suddenly I heard a thud and my husband was on the floor. He was there a long time, started to get up and fell back again and when he finally got back into his seat he was so drunk on the power of God, he hardly knew what was happening. He said it was like he had experienced the most relaxing time of his life and every bone was unhooked. That night will always be a memorial in my life—it showed me a new dimension of power. We have had people fall under the power in our services, we have seen some great moves of the Spirit in our church, but I have never seen such a sovereign move of God. Thank you, thank you for coming our way and giving of yourself so freely as channels for His power. Jesus is so irresistible and I am sure it would have been almost impossible to have resisted Him that night.

One of those who rededicated her life to Christ, received the baptism with the Holy Spirit and was completely 'zapped' by the power of God. She went straight home, gathered up $50.00 worth of ESP books and proceeded to burn them. Hallelujah!!!"

This was one of the most exciting nights of our whole life! Some 1700 jammed the ballroom for a miracle service. The power was so strong it was difficult to stand up. When the tremendous clap ovation for Jesus came, the power swooped down and somewhere around 200 people fell under the power right where they stood! The congregation was predominantly Lutheran and Catholic!

Then things really got exciting! The word of knowledge started working and as we called out healings, we asked them to come to the platform and tell us what happened. Then we made a startling discovery! The power of God was so strong they couldn't get to the microphone! We were both hanging on to the pulpit because it was almost impossible for us to stand. When anyone approached the platform they looked like they had stepped on a banana peel, and down they went, under the power of God! A beautiful Catholic nun tried to get to the mike, but instead fell on the floor, personally touched by the hand of God! We had written about this in our monthly newsletter and today we received a letter which said: "Yesterday I received another letter from you where those approaching the platform were not able to proceed, being overwhelmed by the presence of God, and II Chronicles 7:2 tells of a similar encounter with God:

'And the priests could not enter into the house of the Lord, because the glory of the Lord had filled the Lord's house.'

Praise God that His glory can still fill the temple! And praise God that His power has not lessened one iota!" And when all the children of Israel saw how the fire came down, and the glory of the Lord upon the house, they bowed themselves with their faces to the ground upon the pavement, and worshipped, and praised the Lord, saying, For he is good; for his mercy endureth for ever." (II Chronicles 7:3 KJV)

If there is anything that will break down preconceived notions, beliefs and ideas, it is watching or participating in a miracle service. God never seems to choose exactly the same way to do the same miracle. And often he does it in a humorous way. The following letter is self explanatory about an unusual way God worked in a couple's life!

"Dearest Beloved Frances and Charles,

"We want to share with you the miracle that has happened in our lives. The joyous miracle happened to my husband that Sunday night at the church in Tacoma. Dennis fell from a ladder (about 20 feet) while working in November 1972. He broke his knee in two places, also his heel. The doctors told him he'd never run again. He was left with a limp. Needless to say how hard it was for Dennis to accept this. Praise God.

At the service that night, Dennis was an UNBE-LIEVER all the way down the aisle. Matter of fact, the only reason he was going down that aisle with me was because of the 'couple' call. (You had invited couples forward to ask Jesus to bless marriages.) However, Praise the Lord, watching God's Holy Spirit move upon the people (starting to make him think) was scaring him to death, and confusion was in his mind all the way, until the final step was near, and we were next! He spoke with Charles first, to my surprise. Charles said to him, 'What do you want Jesus to do for you?" Dennis said, "I hurt my knee falling off a roof last November and the doctors say I'll never be able to run again, and I want to run.' Charles prayed a very short prayer and then said to Dennis, 'Now bend your knee,' and Dennis did, and discovered he could. Then Charles said, 'Now, RUN!' And Praise the Lord, God spoke through Charles to my husband. Like a bolt of lightning he started to run. Praise the Lord! Needless to say I'm left standing with Charles, and Charles didn't even know where he went. After a few minutes, here came my precious husband, sweating and crying, confessing and praying! I'm getting so excited writing this. Then another bolt of lightning! Both of us fell under the power with hands joined as one. The power of the Holy Spirit fell upon us, and oh, the glory of it all!

The joyous feeling that was in our 'one' heart as we left the church was wonderful. (Three months before this, we were planning a divorce.) Our marriage was on a solid rock called Jesus again after 12 years. Praise the Lord!

The second grand and glorious miracle that night, my husband pulled over to the side of the road a mile from home and said, 'Praise the Lord, I'll see you at home.' He started running like a deer through the night, GLORY, GLORY, GLORY!!! I drove on home in amazement.

I've thanked Jesus many times for the pleasure of meeting and knowing another part of His family. You two will forever remain a part of our lives through Jesus Christ our LORD. In Jesus' name, thank you.

(signed) Connie and Dennis"

From Amarillo, Texas, D.P. writes:

"Words cannot express how we feel about what a change has come into our life through you. I'll just start from the first in that we had really drifted in every possible way. We did all the 'in' (?) things except drugs and I guess it was just because they weren't 'in' then. We wanted to be liked and have fun and that was what we did. In January of this year some dear friends gave us PRAISE THE LORD ANYWAY and the way they talked to us we really wanted more in our life. We came home and read that book. Now lots of people have given us books we never read, and my husband hardly ever reads, but we read that and the next day he went to get all of your other books. (At that time THE TWO SIDES OF A COIN wasn't out.) We just couldn't read enough and I would look up every Scripture you mentioned. Then in February we found out you were coming to town. I was so excited and then I prayed asking if it was real that God was talking to me through your books, or was I just looking to the Hunters as my answer. I asked that if it was God that I would have a chance to visit with you alone! Now George had been in California about 10 days when THE TWO SIDES OF A COIN was released so he hadn't read it. I did, and really searched in my Bible, too. When I'd try and talk to George about it he just hit the roof and was not at all receptive but he still knew what your books had done for us (we've joined a church and are just really on fire for the Lord). Anyway when we went Saturday night we were just disgusted, I guess, and I was so confused. To me religion was something serious and all the 'hallelujahing' and 'amening' was all spooky! When we came home I was just sick—first I was confused because I just loved you so much. I have never been emotional but I cried all night. I really prayed for answers and boy, did we read in Acts, and all the things you said and did were right there in the Bible. George told me to go Sunday but he wouldn't go with me so I really prayed if this was God's work that George would come. When I was on my way out the door he said, 'Wait a minute, I know I'll be miserable if I don't go.' We got there and for no reason (or God's reason I should say) we went to the fellowship hall and there you were. We went right over to talk to you and when we waited awhile and were fixing to walk off, you said, 'Charles, this couple wants to talk to us,' and Frances, my prayer was answered and it was all so very real. George and I both felt different. We really felt that service. I was fighting the prayer language and George still thought if you spoke in tongues you hollered and screamed and rolled on the floor. When you touched us we went down under the power of Jesus. It was beautiful! When we left and came home we were so relaxed and exhausted—we both napped, which is unusual. Then Thursday night I told George I wanted the prayer language so I could have an even closer relationship with God and the next thing I knew George had called you and you know the rest [they both received the baptism and began speaking in tongues]. We pray both ways, but it is very special and like I said I've never been emotional but I just have tears rolling down my face as I talk. Also the hardest thing for me was to put Jesus first and George and my two children next, and I'm still praying on it, and when I do His love surrounds me so much I can't talk . . . only tears."

From a Texas Methodist businesswoman:

"Bart and I have been married for 15 years, have three children, and attend church on a somewhat irregular basis. We have been invited by the Hunters to attend fellowship meetings several times but have never made it to them. A good friend of ours who suffers from arthritis asked us to go with her to a special meeting held in a motel at which she hoped to receive alleviation from her illness. Of course, we both agreed to go with her.

As the time arrived and we drove up to the motel, both Bart and I were wondering what we had got ourselves into. We had heard of the miracles of healing, the speaking in tongues and being 'slain in the Spirit' that seemed to accompany Mr. and Mrs. Hunter wherever they spoke of Jesus. It had all sounded very fine. But now that we were to see these things ourselves and be a part of it all, we both experienced a sudden attack of 'butterflies.' In fact, my husband suggested he drop us off and go get some coffee in a restaurant until we were ready to leave. I asked him to please come in with me and lend his moral support. We found seats at the back of the room and looked around a little uneasily.

Right away we were surprised at how happy and friendly the people were and that many seemed to be 'businessmen-types' there with their families. I don't really know what we expected but somehow we were comforted to see people just like ourselves.

When the meeting started we became more and more at ease. Since we did not know the songs at first we looked around at the singers and were amazed at the joy, happiness and love on everyone's face as they sang of their love to Jesus. It was very moving and before long we also raised our arms and looked upward and sang the simple songs of faith and love. Since I had not heard Bart sing in our entire married life, this was a small but very real miracle to me! He always stands up and opens his hymn book but doesn't open his mouth. I told him afterwards that I hadn't realized he had such a nice voice. God blessed our marriage that night and our love for each other seemed to be renewed and flowed out for each of us to see, and I felt like a bride again."

From Ohio, B.G. writes: (she had attended the Pittsburgh Charismatic Convention).

"WOW! What a week! I don't see how anyone could ever be the same after a week like that. Especially when it's the first time I ever really worshipped God like I felt inside. Something finally let go and there is now so much more freedom than I felt before.

Thursday evening was the highlight of the week for me. I would like to try to tell you exactly what happened. I don't know if everyone feels the same when slain in the Spirit, but here goes.

I really had no idea what to expect when I stepped out to you that night. You laid hands on me and since I didn't realize your first words would be your prayer I was looking at you until I heard, 'Father.' Then I closed my eyes and really joined in that prayer. You prayed and then I believe you said, 'bless her,' and through your hands from God came the most beautiful sensation I have ever felt in my entire life. It started from where your hands were and went down through every cell of my body. I really wish there were words to describe it, but somehow I know you know. I was very aware of going backwards and thinking they really don't need to catch me, I'll just float down. I was aware of everything going on around me, but not really caring; just an overwhelming sense of praise and peacefulness. It's still there! I would like to have laid there forever, but became aware of the fact you were coming back and I'd better move. I finally sat up but was too weak to get the rest of the way up. I looked around on the floor and praise the Lord, there were bodies everywhere. Finally I managed on rubbery legs to get back to my seat. It wasn't very long until the flood gates opened and the tears poured. I'll never be the same!"

Mrs. G.A. of Seattle, Washington writes: "My husband and I had the privilege of enjoying your sharing and miracle service at John Knox Presbyterian Church in Seattle on April 26th. We both got 'slain under the power' and if we ever get a chance to get 'slain' again believe me, we will! Why not? It's a free gift from the Lord, isn't it? It doesn't cost a thing, does it? Why do people hesitate to receive the gifts? Some of my friends from our church came running up to me after I came down off the platform that night and asked me what was it like? I said 'It was the most beautiful experience of my life.' To have Jesus touch you and be completely at His mercy, unable to move, just lying there and being flooded with waves and waves of His love for just me, only me, a one to one thing. I told them to go up and get some too, it was free!!!! Well, they didn't, they were too chicken. Praise the Lord anyway."

From Alabama, A.L. writes:

"Thank you so much for your letter of May 3rd stating that you would see me at the Full Gospel Fellowship meeting in Atlanta. Well, I did see you, and I was 'slain' under the power and I saw many miracles happen. Two miracles happened right in our group of seven who had traveled over 200 miles to be there for the breakfast.

A friend of mine employs a deaf and dumb man in her engineering business. She took him over for a healing and he was HEALED! He has not had any speech lessons yet but he turns on his car radio to hear the programs and is also trying to talk. He also vomited every time he tried to smoke after your prayer at that breakfast.

Another healing occurred to this same friend's 84 year old mother. She could not hear with two hearing aids on—now, she doesn't even wear one and she hears the clock ticking in her bedroom."

Author's note: About the third person prayed for at the Full Gospel meeting was the deaf mute. On the way up to Atlanta, we had read the Scripture where the deaf mute was healed. God impressed on my mind what Jesus said. I repeated exactly the same words, "You deaf and dumb spirit come out of this man right now in the name of Jesus!" We were all instantly aware that something had happened because the man (35 years old) kept pointing to his ears and then to his head. I kept whispering in his ear, "Say PRAISE THE LORD," and all of a sudden he looked at me, and the first words he ever spoke came out sounding like, "Pwaise." Remember one who has been a deaf mute has to be taught how to speak. Next I tried to get him to say, "Jesus" and he came out with some sound which was hard to distinguish, but he made a noise anyway. The crowd shouted, "Hallelujah" and "Amen" and all of a sudden he turned to me and said, "Amen!" in that funny, flat sounding voice that accompanies most deafness. The tears really flowed!

131

Three weeks after this letter was received we were with the employer of this man. She reports he is "jabbering like a baby" as he is learning to talk. And how he understood about smoking, we'll never know except the Spirit of God communicated with him. The power of God is truly an awesome thing!

Who understands why some people are INSTANTLY healed and others have healings which take a longer time? God proves his versatility in doing healings of all kinds so that we will never think we completely understand how He works, because who knows the mind of God? The following letter shows two very unique healings in one family—done in different ways!

"Dear Frances and Charles,

Jeanie and I are Seniors at Stephen F. Austin State University. We were with you at the F.G.B.M.F.I. in Beaumont.

Just before you were to speak at the Ladies' Luncheon, Jeanie stopped you as you approached the platform. She was quite nervous and had picked her cuticles until tiny drops of blood had appeared. She asked you to pray for her. You did, and immediately it was time for her to play another song for the soloist. Then, Praise Jesus, we noticed while she was playing the piano that the Lord was healing her cuticles right before our eyes. Well you can imagine our excitement, Hallelujah! Jeanie turned to me and said, 'Honey, go have her pray for that growth on your neck while the anointing of God is on her.'

I have had a complexion problem ever since I was in the seventh grade and for five years I was under a dermatologist's care in Tyler. This cyst came up on my neck (just under my shirt collar) at age 13. The doctor said that it was of no major importance but it would have to be removed surgically.

This year I am 23 years old and the cyst had grown to the size of a hen egg. Jeanie was quite concerned in the fact that it was growing.

I came forward for you to pray for it and these were your exact words: 'Oh, thank you, Jesus, for another opportunity to show your mighty power. Bless Him, Father and heal this growth. I curse it in the name of Jesus.'

Guess what! I went out under the power. When I got up you felt the cyst, and nothing happened. You told me to thank Jesus because he was going to take it away ('Go on your way rejoicing, believing it's done!') So I did. That was on Good Friday, the 20th of April, and exactly one week later on Great Friday, April 27th, at about 12:00 midnight, Jeanie and I were sitting in the living room just sharing Jesus when all of a sudden the place on my neck began to itch. I went into the bathroom to look at it in the mirror. I squeezed it and a handful of dead old tissue came out through a tiny hole in the skin. It literally exploded! Praise Jesus! That was the end of my growth that I had carried around for 10 years.

I had sung 'He Touched Me' many times before, but never like I can now. All praise be unto Jesus. We love Him. Since then Jesus has opened so many doors for us to people we thought impossible to reach. They just can't say anything when you have a real live miracle.

Jeanie and I are Southern Baptists. We are music director and church pianist at a small church in Texas. Jeanie has not picked her cuticles since then. This was also a nervous habit that I had acquired in elementary school and when I saw that Jeanie was healed, I asked her to pray for me. (We were in the car coming back from the convention.) Praise Jesus, my cuticles have healed and my small case of nerves is gone too. I'm so glad that Jesus cares even about the little things in our marriage so that He could always keep us one flesh!

There are times when we feel we haven't been healed right when WE wanted to be healed, but praise God the healing really did take place—it was just 7 days later than we anticipated!"

Many of the letters we received after miracle services are interesting and informative. We want to share a few with you.

T.D.P. of California wrote: "I was an usher and received great blessings by helping and watching first hand. I fell under the power and He firmly planted me on the Rock (Jesus) to serve and thank with joy forever. While under the power I received the baptism of the Holy Spirit. My left leg which was shorter than the right, was lengthened as God healed my back. Charles and Frances laid hands on me for special service and the first person I ever prayed for to receive the baptism immediately received."

KLY, JR. of Youngstown, Ohio writes:

"I was a very skeptical person about the power of healing. I became a believer when a member of our church who was confined to a wheelchair for approximately ten years (he was a paraplegic) received Jesus Christ into his life and through the Lord, he got up from the wheelchair and is now walking and doing very well—Praise the Lord!

A few months ago when you visited Tabernacle United Presbyterian Church, I attended your meeting with only one intention. I am a Deacon in the church, and thought I could help with the crowd by seating people, etc.

I was called upon to assist at the rail, as persons received the Holy Spirit. I was amazed at the number of people who came forward and with my own eyes I saw many of them healed.

Toward the end of the evening, my wife and a member of our church asked me if I would go forward and ask for a healing.

I don't know what it was, but it must have been a push from Jesus, as I walked forward and went up to Mr. Hunter and asked for a healing of my left foot and my high blood pressure. After a few minutes of prayer, you touched me, and through Jesus Christ, the Spirit descended on me, and I was flat on my back. I heard you pray that my foot be healed and that I have movement in my toes, and my blood pressure be lowered.

After several minutes I got up from the floor and started to walk around. I flexed my toes, in which I had no movement for over 20 years, and all pain was gone! I was able to move my large left toe and flex my other toes. To this day, which is over two months from your visit, I have had no pain, can put pressure on my feet and move my toes. Praise the Lord!

For skeptics who doubt the power of healing, my doctors can attest to my disability as a result of my large toe being broken three times and calcium deposits being in the joints of my toes. My Army discharge will also attest to my disability."

K.U. writes: "I received a miracle healing because the Lord did a double lengthening in my arm. The one that was long got longer and the short one got just as long as the other one. Charles said there was an ear healing where I was sitting. He said, 'Glory,' and it sounded like he was yelling! It was I who received the hearing. Praise God. When I fell under the power He gave me a peace I have never had and I started laughing at the top of my voice (holy laughter)."

F.L.L. (age 17) writes: "I have had back trouble for many months. The doctor said it was a muscle problem. Exercises were suggested but didn't seem to be helping. When Charles said, 'There has been a back problem healed over here,' and pointed to my section of the church, I realized my back didn't hurt any more. It was relaxed and felt good! I jumped up and said, 'It's me, it's me!' I could touch my toes with no strain. Thank you, Jesus!!!! Frances was right when she said 'you're never the same after God touches you.' "

Hallelujah!

It's hard to close each chapter in this book because each day brings more exciting letters and phone calls about the awesomeness of God's power, so we decided this book just could never end, but would have to be continued in another book. We couldn't close though, without letting you read a copy of a letter just received in this morning's mail.

"I am writing to tell you of a healing I received on May 17, 1973, through your ministry at the Pittsburgh Charismatic Conference. Praise the Lord!

On May 15 I had been told by my doctor, Richard C. Snyder, that I had a nodule in my breast and that the nodule would definitely have to be removed surgically for further examination. He referred me to Dr. David Orsinger, likewise a local physician and surgeon, for further testing and to set up the date for surgery. When Dr. Orsinger was unable to detect the nodule by an office examination, he asked me to go to the Pittsburgh Diagnostic Clinic for X-rays, just to make certain. This I gladly did, at which time Dr. David Huot could find no evidence of a nodule in an office examination. And of course the X-rays showed that the nodule had disappeared!

I give all thanks and praise to our Lord Jesus Christ for this healing. Charles was the vessel Jesus used, but the glory belongs to Jesus. I do appreciate the yieldedness and the surrendered life of the vessel, and I believe that our Lord is able to use the two of you in such a powerful way because your marriage is truly in Him and you are in divine order. It was an inspiration for many of us who have Christian mates.

The thing that perhaps touched me the most is that Jesus had time for me, on that busy night when hundreds were pressing in for healing. It was a needed assurance for me that I am valuable to Him, and I praise and thank Him for this amazing fact. Also, He arranged it so that I personally felt the nodule and knew that it was real before the healing. Isn't He wonderful?

These medical facts are a matter of record. If any more details are needed, I will be happy to help."

Thank you, Jesus! Thank you, Jesus! Thank you, Jesus! This was a fabulous night at the Pittsburgh Charismatic Conference as an estimated thousand individuals went under the power! It was so crowded, people pressed forward in waves to touch two ordinary people. Praise God they didn't see either of us, but only Jesus living in and through us.

Every day we are convinced more and more that the Power of God is an awesome thing. Who can understand how something that you can't see can bring a person out of a wheelchair; make the deaf to hear; heal cancer, make the blind to see and deliver a dope addict instantly. And yet it does. Last week a man simply got out of his wheelchair and said, "You can have this, I'll never need it again!" There was no lightning, no thunder, no nothing you could smell, feel or touch, but because of the awesomeness of God's power a miracle happened. Lord Jesus, may we never become used to your power. May we never fail to be thrilled when your glory fills the temple!

Chapter 9

LET JESUS COME ALIVE!!!

We just hung up the telephone from someone who said, "My mother was at one of your meetings a week ago Saturday and she came home on such a spiritual mountaintop she said, 'Don't anybody talk to me—I just want to worship God the rest of the day!' " This is what this great Holy Spirit revival is doing to people—they want to worship God!!! Never in the history of Christianity has the name Jesus been on the lips of so many as it is today. Never before have so many become so intimately acquainted with the Son of God. Never before have people worshipped God openly as they do today.

A businessman who is very distinguished, successful, rich, intelligent, educated, cultured and refined, recently said something that went home to our hearts. He was sharing his personal testimony of how he found Christ and the struggle that followed after that as he attempted to make Jesus REAL in his life. He had gone from one church to another, seeking a fulfillment of what he had wanted in his heart, and had found nothing adequate to meet his needs. He didn't know what it was that was lacking, but he knew it had to be somewhere, so he kept on searching. One day he went to a Kathryn Kuhlman Miracle Service and saw the one thing that triggered him toward the answer to his quest. He said, "That was the first time I had ever seen people honestly 'worshipping' God, and I knew this was what was lacking in my life. Openly and unashamedly making love to God in perfect adoration and worship, and I knew it was what I needed to fulfill my life."

This is what the Holy Spirit is doing today as He sweeps across the world! He is wooing people into a real love relationship with Jesus! And as hearts are opening up, God is pouring out His Spirit more and more. We are beginning to fulfill the purpose for which we were put on this earth—to have fellowship with God! We're falling in love with Jesus! Jesus is breaking all the fetters. A recent letter states "When I was slain in the Spirit, I recall lying there and my heart broke into small pieces and the bands surrounding it were broken." Hallelujah, people are being set free!

There is a hungering among the clergy that is thrilling to behold! Some of the things that occur during an outpouring of God's Holy Spirit are not exactly what has been going on over the years in many churches, but the desire to really be caught up in this exciting move is overwhelming. In Wichita, Kansas, recently we asked for every member of the clergy to come forward who wanted to have his ministry anointed. The response completely took our breath away as between 50 and 75 pastors accompanied by their wives came forward. We could hardly believe our eyes, because it looked like God's Holy Spirit had literally jerked them out of their seats. There was no holding back, waiting to see what a fellow clergyman was going to do. They almost ran forward to the stage of the beautiful Century II Civic Center. We prayed, asking God to so anoint them and their ministries that their churches would never be the same again. They stood there, Methodist, Presbyterian, Nazarene, Brethren, Mennonite, Assembly of God, Foursquare, Baptist, Congregational, Christian, Friends, Interdenominational pastors, and many others, all wanting everything God had for them. It was a beautiful sight to behold as EVERY SINGLE PASTOR AND HIS WIFE WENT UNDER THE POWER OF GOD!!!! God is moving by His Spirit! Just prior to this, we had noticed 5 Catholic sisters in the congregation, and had asked them to come forward. They all 5 held hands, and we thanked God for what he is doing in the Catholic Churches. When we finished praying, we merely said, "Jesus bless these sisters," and all 5 of them gently fell backwards to the floor at exactly the same time as the Power touched them simultaneously.

The next week in Camp Hill, Pennsylvania, saw the same story re-enacted as we asked the clergy and their wives to come forward. Praise God again for the way He is touching the newspaper reporters, because we quote from the Patriot-News, Harrisburg, Pa. Sunday, Sept. 2, 1973: "It was an afternoon of amazing happenings, the like of which the Penn Harris Motor Inn, in Camp Hill, will probably not see again for a long time. Yesterday afternoon, the next-to-the-final session of the Full Gospel Business Men's Fellowship regional convention headlined Charles and Frances Hunter and under their ministerings, the huge crowd in the ballroom witnessed miracles and manifestations of spiritual power. The matinee was a fitting climax to the convention, for the events of the first Pentecost were re-enacted with miracles, speaking in tongues and 'falling under the power of God.'

"Catholic sisters, ministers and their wives, and priests were invited by the Hunters to stand in front of the platform and receive the 'power of God into their lives.'

"Several sisters and priests and about 50 ministers and wives responded. The Hunters came down to where the religious leaders were and lightly touched each one, calling for power to come into each one's life. As the touch was administered, nearly everyone fell back onto the floor and some couldn't arise for a while.

"One priest described the experience as though an 'ethereal splendor' had come over him and a minister said he had never before experienced such a feeling of 'perfect peace.' "

In Hartford, Connecticut, a Catholic priest came to one of our meetings and received the baptism with the Holy Spirit. He fell under the power and came up from the floor so fired up he just couldn't be held back. He came to each of our services and before long was ministering right along with us. People were being healed as he prayed and fell backwards to the floor as God used him to touch them! Hallelujah!!!

In New Jersey, two Episcopalian and one Catholic priest, an Assembly of God and an American Baptist minister came forward. They all went under the power. The American Baptist said he had not received the baptism, but upon asking to be filled, instantly received. Within 5 minutes he was laying hands on people, seeing them healed and falling backwards under the Power! The fields are white unto harvest, but the laborers are few, and God is using every single one who is willing to jump into the stream of the Living Water!

The momentum continues to grow. What good does this do? The results that come back to us are breathtaking. One pastor reported more than 100 came to the altar at his church the next morning after he had been anointed for special service and had fallen under the Power. Another reported more than 40 came to the altar of his church which had had barren altars for quite some time. Praise God when preaching can become so anointed the Holy Spirit can really move in a church!

A leader in a Southern Baptist Church attended one of our meetings and as God's Holy Spirit began moving, she witnessed people falling under the Power and came forward saying, "I just don't believe this, I just don't believe this!" We gently touched her and said, "Spirit of unbelief, come out right now in the name of Jesus!" She went under the power, and after about 30 minutes, she sat up, turned to the congregation and said "I don't think I was even saved before, but NOW I KNOW I AM!!!!" Praise God because one little supernatural touch of His Power accomplished a BIG miracle!

God is also using the laymen all over the country. After one of our recent meetings a young woman wrote: "I attended a Hunter meeting for the first time last night. I've never seen anything like it before in my life. The first time you asked Jesus' blessing for a man and he fell back on the floor, I nearly collapsed from shock.

"A lady in her sixties sitting next to me had a roaring in her ears and had a hard time hearing you during the program. When Charles said that those with hearing problems would be healed, she was healed right on the spot, before she even had a chance to stand up.

"To give you some idea of my background, I was raised as a Presbyterian. The only time I heard of the Holy Ghost was in the Doxology and then He was an it, not a He. He was not a person of God, only an it that I didn't understand. God has been leading me along the road of spiritual development, knowing just when to introduce me to new things along the way. Last night was one of those introductions.

"For some time I have been trying to figure out why I lacked power to witness. I knew that I lacked something, but I didn't know what. As I sat there last night a voice came into my head saying 'she will know what you lack and you will receive what you need.' Well, I thought He meant Frances. I went up on the stage with a 'here goes nothing' attitude. I didn't really believe that anyone was going to knock me over. I kept waiting to speak to Frances but she was busy, then suddenly a little lady with the most beautiful light in her eyes came up to me and asked why I was there and I told her. She said, 'You need joy and boldness, and you shall have it,' then she took my hands and prayed for me. As she was praying I said in my mind, 'Jesus, if this isn't you I'm going to plant my feet firmly so only a hard shove could knock me over.' Then the lady touched my forehead so very lightly and all of a sudden I was floating. I still can't believe it happened although I know it did. WOW! I felt like I received a shot in the arm. I could whip my way through lions."

Praise God He is using laymen from all denominations and all walks of life as well as pastors. The "little lady with the most beautiful light in her eyes" ministers along with her husband at each of our home prayer meetings! And look what happened to a first-timer. She went away feeling like she could whip her way through lions. Hallelujah! God is breaking down all barriers of all kinds as the Spirit sweeps magnificently and tirelessly across the nation and around the world!

Never in history has there been such a hungering for the Word of God! Never before has a Bible been such a commonplace item. Today you'll notice people of all ages, all denominations, in all walks of life, carrying them under their arms. Never before has there been such a demand for exciting Bible teaching. People like Judson Cornwall, Don Basham, Derek Prince, Charles Simpson, Malcolm Smith, to name a few, and there are many, many others, could be teaching every single day of the year, and drawing tremendous crowds if they could physically stand it. People are hungering and thirsting for righteousness as never before in history. The sale of all translations of the Bible is phenomenal! Cassette tape recorders are part of the standard equipment of almost all Christians as they tape the messages and then replay them to their friends. The way cassette tapes are sent back and forth across the world is astounding! Not only just across our nation, but around the world where missionaries and servicemen are hungry for up-to-the-minute messages! People are finding time to listen to top teachers all throughout the week via cassette tapes. Video tapes are moving out rapidly as a means of teaching in prayer groups and churches!

Never before have people openly talked about Jesus the way they are doing today! The saying used to be "Never discuss politics or religion" and today's Christian world has discovered this isn't in the Bible at all. The name Jesus is a by-word in many households. Many charismatic organizations, such as the Women's AGLOW are literally bursting at the seams and exploding as new chapters spring up daily across the country, full of hungry people who want to talk about Jesus! People who want the fullness of the Spirit!

Never has it been as exciting to be a Christian as it is today. God's Holy Spirit is making it so. People who have never experienced a personal relationship with Jesus Christ are discovering He's real. People who have looked upon "religion" with disinterest, have discovered that Jesus still gives the kind of peace that "passeth understanding." He is still healing the brokenhearted, and He is still in the miracle business. Recently someone in a hospital said, "I don't want a preacher to hold my hand and tell me how to die, I want a preacher who can pray that I'll be healed!" This is one of the best statements I've ever heard made about this Holy Ghost explosion. People want the real thing, and the real thing is JESUS!

Two thousand years ago God loved us so much that He gave His only begotten son so that "anyone who believes in him shall not perish but have eternal life." (John 3:16) Such a simple beautiful truth that is available to all today. God willingly let His Son die and shed His blood on a cross that we might have eternal life! The first seven verses of the book of John 3 sum it up more beautifully than anything ever written:

"After dark one night a Jewish religious leader named Nicodemus, member of the sect of the Pharisees, came for an interview with Jesus, 'Sir,' he said, 'we all know that God has sent you to teach us. Your miracles are proof enough of this.'

144

"Jesus replied, 'With all the earnestness I possess I tell you this: Unless you are born again, you can never get into the Kingdom of God.'

"Born again!' exclaimed Nicodemus. 'What do you mean? How can an old man go back into his mother's womb and be born again?'

"Jesus replied, 'What I am telling you so earnestly is this: Unless one is born of water and the Spirit, he cannot enter the Kingdom of God. Men can only reproduce human life, but the Holy Spirit gives new life from heaven; so don't be surprised at my statement that you must be born again!' "

We never talk without giving people an opportunity to be born again. We couldn't write a book without giving every reader a chance to be born again. It's so easy because it requires just a simple little prayer. Pray it, will you?

"Lord Jesus, forgive my sins. I open the door of my life and invite you to come in. Wash me and cleanse me of all unrighteousness. I turn my back on sin and want to follow you the rest of my life. Come into my heart and live your life through me. Make me the kind of a person you want me to be. Now I thank you for forgiving my sins and for coming into my heart as you promised. Jesus, I love you."

Welcome into God's Royal Family because now you are a child of God!

"And He pointed out to me a river of pure Water of life, clear as crystal, flowing from the throne of God and the Lamb, coursing down the center of the mainstreet. On each side of the river grew Trees of Life, bearing twelve crops of fruit, with a fresh crop each month; the leaves were used for medicine to heal the nations. There shall be nothing in the city which is evil; for the throne of God and of the Lamb will be there, and his servants will worship him. And they shall see his face; and his name shall be written on their foreheads. And there will be no night there—no need for lamps or sun—for the Lord God will be their light; and they shall reign forever and ever." (Rev. 22:1-5)

145

"Then he instructed me 'Do not seal up what you have written, for the time of fulfillment is near. And when that time comes, all doing wrong will do it more and more; the vile will become more vile; good men will be better; those who are holy will continue on in greater holiness.' (Rev. 22:10-11)

"The Spirit and the bride say, 'Come.' Let each one who hears them say the same, 'Come.' Let the thirsty one come—anyone who wants to; let him come and drink the Water of Life without charge." (Rev. 22:17)

Maranatha! Come Lord Jesus! Soon!

THE HUNTER FOUNDATION

A few years ago, Frances entered a hospital known as the "home of the pampered patients!" And it was! A little bag of goodies was given to her with hand cream for her hands, elbow cream for her elbows, heel cream for her heels, lotion for her body, dusting powder to make her smell good—everything for her physical comfort—but nothing for her soul!

She often says, "If I had died that night, I would have spent eternity in hell."

A burning desire was formed in her heart to do something about this. When she and Charles were married, their desires merged to give, free, a life-changing book to hospital patients. How could this be accomplished? God said, "My people will do it for you!"

The Hunter Foundation, which God said is really YOUR foundation, has been established to distribute books free to patients entering hospitals in every city and state in the United States, and hopefully in the world.

For information on how you can have your own personal ministry, either by distribution or contribution, contact:

THE HUNTER FOUNDATION
Box 55810
Houston, TX 77055

Authors and publisher have waived all royalties and profits on the hospital edition of this book.